T0312269

Cambridge Elements ≡

Elements in Corpus Linguistics
edited by
Susan Hunston
University of Birmingham

ANALYSING LANGUAGE, SEX AND AGE IN A CORPUS OF PATIENT FEEDBACK

A Comparison of Approaches

Paul Baker
Lancaster University

Gavin Brookes
Lancaster University

CAMBRIDGE
UNIVERSITY PRESS

CAMBRIDGE
UNIVERSITY PRESS

University Printing House, Cambridge CB2 8BS, United Kingdom

One Liberty Plaza, 20th Floor, New York, NY 10006, USA

477 Williamstown Road, Port Melbourne, VIC 3207, Australia

314–321, 3rd Floor, Plot 3, Splendor Forum, Jasola District Centre,
New Delhi – 110025, India

103 Penang Road, #05–06/07, Visioncrest Commercial, Singapore 238467

Cambridge University Press is part of the University of Cambridge.

It furthers the University's mission by disseminating knowledge in the pursuit of education, learning, and research at the highest international levels of excellence.

www.cambridge.org
Information on this title: www.cambridge.org/9781009013772
DOI: 10.1017/9781009031042

First published 2022

A catalogue record for this publication is available from the British Library.

ISBN 978-1-009-01377-2 Paperback
ISSN 2632-8097 (online)
ISSN 2632-8089 (print)

Analysing Language, Sex and Age in a Corpus of Patient Feedback

A Comparison of Approaches

Elements in Corpus Linguistics

DOI: 10.1017/9781009031042
First published online: July 2022

Paul Baker
Lancaster University

Gavin Brookes
Lancaster University

Author for correspondence: Paul Baker, j.p.baker@lancaster.ac.uk

Abstract: This Element explores approaches to locating and examining social identity in corpora with and without the aid of demographic metadata. This is a key concern in corpus-aided studies of language and identity and this Element sets out to explore the main challenges and affordances associated with each approach and to discern what they can (and cannot) show. It describes two case studies, which each compare two approaches to social identity variables – sex and age – in a corpus of 14 million words of patient comments about NHS cancer services in England. The first approach utilises demographic tags to group comments according to patients' sex/age, while the second involves categorising cases where patients disclose their sex/age in their comments. This Element compares the findings from both approaches, which are critically discussed in terms of their implications for corpus-aided studies of language and identity.

Keywords: cancer, language, corpus, sex, age

ISBNs: 9781009013772 (PB), 9781009031042 (OC)
ISSNs: 2632-8097 (online), 2632-8089 (print)

Contents

1 Introduction

1.1 Introduction and Aims

In recent years, researchers working in areas of linguistics such as applied linguistics, sociolinguistics and discourse studies have increasingly harnessed methods from corpus linguistics to examine the relationship between language use and social identity. Corpus linguistics is a collection of methods but also a field of research that involves analysing language use based on large collections of naturally occurring language data (McEnery and Wilson, 2001). This dataset is known as a corpus (pl. corpora). Corpora are designed to be representative of a particular language or language variety and are analysed using computational techniques that help analysts to identify and interpret frequent or salient aspects of language use. While computers aid the focus of such analyses, it is the job of the human analyst to move beyond the computer output and to interpret and explain the linguistic patterns in their corpora.

Corpus methods have, as noted, witnessed increasing take-up in linguistic studies of social identity in recent years. As we will see in this section, much of this work has used corpora that are annotated or 'tagged' for socio-demographic information about the people who contribute the language or texts to the corpus (see Baker, 2010; see also the recent collections by Brezina et al., 2018 and Friginal, 2018). While advancements in corpus annotation have unquestionably increased the possibilities for undertaking corpus-aided research of language and identity (Kendall, 2011), the use of annotation in such studies is by no means ubiquitous. Indeed, there remain, as we will see, instances where such annotation has not been used, as well as cases where it is simply not possible to annotate a corpus for socio-demographic information. In such cases more manual approaches to identifying and analysing social identity are often used. The aim of this Element is to compare these two broad approaches to identifying and analysing identity in corpora. To do this, we analyse social identity in language use in a corpus of patient comments on cancer care services in the UK. We will approach this data from two methodological perspectives: one using socio-demographic metadata and the other taking a more data-driven approach based on cases where particular aspects of identity (sex and age) are occasioned in the discourse through patients mentioning them in the language they use in their comments.

This section consists of five sub-sections. Following this brief introduction, we focus on the concept of identity, consider how it relates to language use and outline our theoretical perspective on this relationship. We then discuss existing approaches to studying language and identity in corpora, in particular those that employ the use of socio-demographic metadata annotation. The final sub-section describes the data and corpus linguistic techniques we use in our analysis over the next two sections.

1.2 Sex, Gender and Age

In this sub-section we provide definitions for the variables analysed in this Element.

First, we address the tricky distinction between *sex* and *gender*. The term 'gender' has an overlapping but not identical meaning to 'sex', and the words are sometimes used interchangeably (Udry, 1994). Gender typically refers to differences in male and female behaviour and roles or a person's internal identification of their identity. Sex, meanwhile, refers to the anatomy of a person's reproductive system along with secondary sexual characteristics such as body hair (Kimmel, 2000; Baker, 2008). As such, while sex reflects biological understandings (men and women), gender is concerned with social or cultural understandings of sex roles (maleness and femaleness). The data we analyse in this Element is categorised by sex (based on patient records) and so when we speak of finding sex differences we refer to the comparison of these two categories. However, it is also important to note that we will relate similarities and differences in language use between the sexes to *gendered* discourses, that is, ways of making sense of and communicating about the world with respect to gender (Sunderland, 2004; Baker, 2008). For example, a patient may state that they are male (referring to their sex) and note that because of this they feel unable to express pain. We would view this as a gendered discourse, relating to expectations about how men should behave.

Ageing can be defined as the combination of biological, psychological and social processes that affect people as they grow older (Harris, 2007). Age is an extremely salient aspect of social life, with different ages marking new stages of life (e.g. starting school, marriage, retirement). Coupland notes the importance of age in social interaction.

> [A]ge identity is often nearer to the surface of talk and text than other dimensions of social identification. There are very many social encounters where age is made immediately and obviously salient, and where it becomes a thematic resource for talk. In most public encounters between nonacquaintances, gender, race, and class will be covertly negotiated, and their salience and consequentiality will be difficult to read at the surface of talk. But age-work ... is often overt, for example, in the actual telling of age in years ... or in talk about social or personal change. (Coupland, 2004: 84)

For this analysis, we quantify patients' ages in years. The reasons for this are threefold. First, our previous research on patient feedback has found these types of age disclosures to be the most frequent in this genre, thereby giving us the largest amount of data to analyse when we use patients' age self-references. Second, this approach is more reliable than relying on instances where age is implied but not stated explicitly (e.g. patients may use terms such as 'middle-aged' inconsistently). Third, and finally, this approach allowed us to develop a consistent set of search terms that could be applied across all age groups under study and, crucially, that could be compared with the age-related demographic metadata accompanying the comments, which also gave patients' ages in years (discussed in Section 1.4).

The patient survey data that we analyse in this Element was divided into eight age groups, with the lowest being sixteen to twenty-four and the oldest being eighty-five plus. There is no ideal way of categorising age and we acknowledge that different age boundaries are likely to produce new or even different findings. It is beyond the scope of this Element to carry out a comparison of every age group, so in Section 3 we have focussed on a comparison of the two age groups that contained the most data (sixty-five to seventy-four years and seventy-five to eighty-four years).

While the analysis in this Element is focussed on just two variables – sex and age – the techniques outlined over the forthcoming sections could (and should) be used to investigate a much wider range of socio-demographic variables, for example ethnicity, sexuality, religion, income level or education level and we hope that this Element will inspire further research in a wide range of identity variables.

1.3 Language and Identity

The topic of identity has long been of interest to researchers in the social sciences and humanities. Preece (2016), in her introduction to the *Routledge Handbook of Language and Identity*, argues that researchers are interested in identity 'because it enables the gap between the micro level of the individual and the macro level of the social order to be bridged. It allows for the investigation of an individual's membership of particular groups, affiliations to cultural customs and practices and representations of self and others' (2016: 3). Despite the great interest in identity within (and beyond) the social sciences and humanities, the concept of identity remains notoriously difficult to define. Gleason (1983) points out that the term 'identity' emerged in social science literature during the 1950s, with subsequent studies on the topic tending to fall into one of two broad categories that reflect opposing conceptions. The first approaches identity as 'intrapsychic', that is, as an internal and fixed quality that reflects 'who we really are'. The second approaches identity as a socially constructed role that is acquired or even imposed. Between the two poles is Habermas's (1979) notion of ego identity, which represents a socialised sense of individuality (see also: Baker, 2010: 10).

Researchers within the social sciences and humanities have increasingly viewed identity in the second sense described by Gleason (1983); that is, from a non-essentialist perspective, as a socially constructed and fluid phenomenon that has multiple dimensions (e.g. age, culture, ethnicity, gender, religion, sexuality, social class and so on). Preece (2016: 3) describes a shift in applied linguistic studies 'from viewing identity as a set of fixed characteristics that are learned or biologically based to seeing identity as a social construct'. This shift reflects the ever-complex nature of identity that has resulted from the increasing 'mobility and diversity that has arisen in the social worlds of the physical and digital due to the processes of globalisation in late modernity' (Preece, 2016: 3).

This shift towards viewing identity as something that is constructed by discourse and other forms of social and embodied conduct is frequently con-ceptualised as a 'discursive' or 'post-modern' turn in the social sciences, humanities and beyond. An aspect of this process that is relevant to linguists and other analysts of discourse is what Benwell and Stokoe (2006: 4) describe as the relocation of identity, 'from the "private" realms of cognition and experience, to the "public" realms of discourse and other semiotic systems of meaning-making'. Consequently, many commentators now argue that 'rather than being reflected in discourse, identity is actively, ongoingly, dynamically constituted in discourse' (Benwell and Stokoe, 2006: 4). For example, Burr (2003: 106) describes identities as being 'constructed out of the discourses culturally available to us, and which we draw upon in our communications with other people' (see also: Butler, 1990; Baxter, 2003).

Adopting a broadly social constructionist view then, there is no 'real' or 'essential' self that hides behind discourse. Rather, analysts working from this perspective set out to examine how individuals' understandings of identity and how any notion of inner or outer selves are 'used rhetorically, to accomplish social action' (Benwell and Stokoe, 2006: 4).

In this Element, we use the term 'identity' in a broadly post-structuralist sense to refer to the various subject positions that social actors construct for themselves and that may also be imparted to them, through discourse and other social activities. We also view identity as something that is subject to change according to context and time, including over the course of an individual's life. We acknowledge the potential for the various subject positions that an individ-ual inhabits to be multiple and fragmented and thus for identity to be a site of struggle. While we would thus orient to a broadly non-essentialist view of identity, we also acknowledge that at a given point some identities may feel and/or be constructed as more authentic and as reflecting our 'real' selves. As in our previous research on discourse and identity (e.g. Baker, 2006; Hunt and Brookes, 2020), we are also sympathetic to the (critical) realist notion that social actors' capacity to construct their identities is subject to social constraints at the micro (i.e. interactional) and macro (i.e. societal) levels.

1.4 Corpus Approaches to Language and Identity

So far we have addressed the issue of identity from a mainly theoretical angle, considering some of the main theories that have guided the ontological status of identity that has been operationalised in research within the social sciences and humanities, including in areas of linguistics such as applied linguistics, socio-linguistics and discourse studies. We have established the tendency within these fields for identity to be viewed as something that is not just located within the individual but that is built, maintained and altered through discourse and other social activities. Now, we turn our attention to more practical considerations. In particular, to how we go about identifying the discursive mechanisms through which identity is constituted. Bucholtz and Hall (2005) present a detailed overview of approaches to identifying and studying discursive mechanisms of identity construction. We will not repeat or attempt to extend their review here. Instead, we will use this space to consider the main approaches that characterise corpus-aided research of language and identity. The approaches and studies discussed in this section adopt an ostensibly diverse range of theoretical per-spectives on identity and how this manifests in language use and so not all of the studies discussed are consistent with the view of identity mapped out in the previous section. Where possible, we have drawn on examples of studies relevant to sex/gender and age, as these are aspects of identity on which our own analysis over the next two sections focusses.

In corpus studies of language and identity, socio-demographic metadata tags are typically used to allocate the language users featured in the corpus into categories that reflect different groups within a given attribute. For example, when investigating sex, language users might be grouped into categories such as male, female, non-binary and so on. Meanwhile, for age the groupings may reflect different age groups such as adolescents, people in their twenties, people in their thirties and so forth. The annotations reflecting these various groupings are then used to divide the corpus into a series of sub-corpora that then form the basis of the analysis, including comparative analyses in which the different groups are compared and contrasted with each other.

The first of the demographic variables we investigate in this Element – sex – has been widely studied in corpus-aided sociolinguistic research, with a plethora of studies making use of the types of large, demographically annotated corpora discussed earlier in this section. While the findings of such work should therefore not be considered as necessarily applying to other languages – or indeed other varieties of English – such studies are at least pertinent to this Element, which similarly focusses on English language data from the UK. An early example is Rayson et al. (1997), who utilised the socio-demographic tags in the spoken section of the 100 million word British National Corpus (BNC) to examine demographic differences in vocabulary use. McEnery et al. (2000) also used the sex-related tags in this corpus to compare the prevalence of swearing and bad language words among men and women. Further examples can be drawn from more recent studies carried out on the spoken component of the 2014 update of the original BNC (i.e. the Spoken BNC 2014), which is also annotated for speakers' demographic information. For example, Fuchs (2017) compared men's and women's use of intensifiers, while Laws et al. (2017) carried out a diachronic analysis of the effects of age and sex on the usage patterns of verb-forming suffixation in this corpus. We should note that not all research in this field focusses on between-sex differences, for example, Baker (2014) carried out a within-sex variation corpus study, analysing a corpus of academic speech to focus on the ways that female academics disagree. Additionally, while many of the studies noted in this Element only focus on one demographic variable at time, this is not always the case. For example McEnery (2005) considers multiple variables together to consider patterns of swearing, although this can be hard to implement due to difficulties in creating perfectly representative spoken corpora, so the more combinations of categories that are considered, the greater the chance for missing data. For more detailed overviews of corpus studies of sex, see Baker (2010; 2014), Murphy (2010) and Baker and Brookes (2021).

In contrast to sex and other social categories such as sexuality and social class, the second variable investigated in this Element – age – has received relatively scant attention from corpus linguists. This is symptomatic of a wider situation within (broadly) sociolinguistic research, in which age has long been rather neglected relative to other social variables (Coupland et al., 1991). However, there are studies that buck this trend, such as the aforementioned studies by Rayson et al. (1997) and Laws et al. (2017), who also considered age alongside sex as variables in their analysis. Most corpus-aided studies of language and age focus on specific age or 'life-stage' groups, which is a controlled variable. Some research in this area, rather than relying on socio-demographic annotation, has analysed corpora sampled from the target age group or from a communicative context designed for that group. For example, Tagliamonte (2016) examined Canadian youth language in computer-mediated communication based on a 179,000-word corpus of computer-mediated texts collected by Tagliamonte's students from among their similarly aged friendship groups. Meanwhile, Harvey and colleagues examined the language of adolescent health discourse by compiling and analysing a corpus of advice-seeking emails submitted to a dedicated adolescent health advice website (Harvey, 2012; Brookes and Harvey, 2016).

The annotation-based approaches that have been used in much corpus-aided sociolinguistic research can be likened to other quantitative social science approaches that seek to correlate social behaviours with macro-identity categories like sex and age. Bucholtz and Hall (2005) note a similar parallel between such social science approaches and the approaches that characterise early variationist sociolinguistic research (Labov, 1966). Likewise, Baker (2010: 8–9) observes how both corpus linguistics and variationist sociolinguistics 'overlap in terms of their epistemology, focus and scope', drawing parallels between them in terms of their 'use of quantitative methodologies in order to carry out comparisons of different populations, focusing on differences and similarities, which can be facilitated with statistical tests', use of 'sampling techniques in order to be able to extrapolate claims to a wider population', their focus on 'variation and change, and … a wide range of linguistic features' and their attempts to 'provide explanations, where possible, for the findings that their research produces'.

In corpus research on identity, as in large-scale variationist sociolinguistic studies, the employment of broad social categories reflected in reliable metadata has proven productive for documenting large-scale sociolinguistic trends. Indeed, the explanatory power of the annotation-based approach arguably rests on the sample of language use being sufficiently large (and representative) to allow statistical correlations to be established between certain social categories and particular forms of language use. Meanwhile, on a more practical level, while annotation may be a labour-intensive task at first, the availability of tags representing social categories of interest can make analysis easier later on, with contrastive analysis of the various resulting identity-based sub-corpora providing a natural 'way in' to the analysis of what may be a very large and otherwise ungainly dataset.

Not all corpus studies take a large-scale, annotation-based approach. Indeed, some studies investigate identity construction without studying the peculiarities of the group(s) under focus, for instance relying instead on the identification of discourses around identity, which are used to construct and (self) attribute identities to particular groups. For example, Stubbs (1996) examined gendered expectations of boys and girls in speeches made by the founder of the Scouts Association, Robert Baden-Powell. His analysis showed that words such as 'happy' and 'happiness' had different collocations and associations depending on whether they were directed at girls (guides) or boys (scouts); guides were instructed to make others happy while scouts were told to focus on their own happiness. Baker (2008: 203–8) compared the discourse surrounding the terms 'bachelor' and 'spinster' in the BNC, finding that although the two words are semantic equivalents (unmarried male and female, respectively), the word spinster tended to accrue negative attributes, such as sexual frustration and unattractiveness, while the word bachelor evidenced comparatively positive attributes for young men, such as being eligible and fun-loving, with older bachelors represented as problematic and their status needing to be 'explained'. The media – especially the print media – has provided a popular data source for corpus-based studies of gendered identity representation. For example, Taylor (2013) compared the use of the terms 'boy' and 'girl' in corpora of British broadsheet newspapers, focussing on similarities as well as differences, while Baker (2014) studied the representation of trans people in a corpus of British newspaper articles.

In studies such as these, demographically tagging the corpus in terms of language users/text producers may not be necessary (or even applicable). However, in other cases reliable socio-demographic metadata may be desirable but not feasible given practical constraints or, depending on the context under study, the corpus compiler's access to the language users under study. For example, reliably annotating a corpus for socio-demographic metadata can also be challenging when dealing with anonymous contexts such as online support groups and other forms of social media. But even in contexts where participants are known, the practice of asking questions to inform annotations can be viewed as intrusive, particularly where the social categories concerned may represent sensitive topics. Accordingly, some corpus studies of language and identity rely on smaller corpora or samples based on identifying instances within the texts in the corpus where language users orient to their identity in the discourse they produce. An example of corpus-aided research on identity that relies on language users' referencing their identity in discourse comes from our previous work on patient feedback language, which serves as the genesis for the research reported in this Element. In Baker et al. (2019), we analysed a corpus of 29 million words of patient comments about the National Health Service (NHS) in England (and 11 million words of provider replies from 2013 to 2015). During the project we worked closely with the NHS, who set us a series of questions that we answered as part of our analysis. One set of questions pertained to the influence of patients' identity on the feedback they gave. Specifically, the NHS wanted us to examine the extent to which patients' sex and age were factors in terms of how they rated a provider quantitatively, as well as the kinds of issues they raised in their comments. However, this question was not straightforward to answer, as the comments provided to us were not accompanied by socio-demographic metadata. This meant that we were not able to annotate our corpus for such information and then carry out targeted, identity-based searches on it or to divide it up into sub-corpora corresponding to different social groups.

We therefore had to find a different way of examining identity in that corpus and the approach we took was to obtain samples of comments by searching for cases where patients explicitly referenced aspects of their identity within their free-text comments. In this way, we explored how these identity categories 'crop up', are 'oriented to' or 'noticed' by the people writing the comments and consider their consequences for the perceptions and evaluations of healthcare given. This approach was loosely inspired by the approaches to 'membership categories' (Sacks, 1995) and 'person reference forms' (Schegloff, 1996) in Conversation Analysis. To find instances where patients referenced their gender or sex, we searched for stretches of text in which either the words 'be', 'is', 'are', 'were' or 'was' were followed by 'man' or 'woman' within the next five words. We then removed false positives (e.g. cases where patients were referring to the sex identity of someone else) and took 100 cases (at random) for male self-identifiers and another 100 cases for female self-identifiers. We then read these 200 pieces of feedback carefully and categorised them in terms of whether they were generally positive or negative and noted the primary theme or driver of the praise or criticism being given. Using this approach we found that the women in our sample provided more negative feedback than the men and that both women and men were each more likely to complain about certain types of issues. To find out whether certain forms of language use were more characteristic of men's or women's comments, we also compared the samples with each other using the keywords technique (introduced in Section 1.5). This revealed gendered differences in feedback style, with women using more personalising language and men tending to present their experiences as generalisations, as well as backing up their points with quantification. In addition, we carried out qualitative analyses of the fifteen mentions of trans, transgender and non-binary identities in the corpus, concluding that sensitivity around one's gender identity is a paramount concern to trans people providing healthcare feedback, with concepts like respect and understanding in relation to gender identity being highly valued.

To identify mentions of age, we experimented with a number of different search-terms and resolved that the most efficient for our purposes was to combine numerical and linguistic references of age together. For example, to search for cases where people mentioned being in their twenties, we used the search-term, '2? Year* old|twenties|20s' (where '|' is an OR operator, '?' allows any number and '*' allows any string of letters in the analytical tool we used, *CQPweb* (Hardie, 2012)). Then, to search for patients in their thirties, we used the search-term, '3? year* old|thirties|30s' and so on, creating seven groups: people aged twenty to twenty-nine, thirty to thirty-nine, forty to forty-nine, fifty to fifty-nine, sixty to sixty-nine, seventy to seventy-nine and eighty to eighty-nine. This search also required some manual checking, so that we could confirm that patients were referring to their own age in their comments. We took all available cases (due to the fact that people did not mention their age very often) and analysed comments manually to categorise them as broadly positive or negative and again to identify recurring themes or drivers of feedback. Our main finding was that satisfaction with the NHS appeared to increase with age, with people in their twenties appearing to be particularly unhappy, being, for example, most likely to complain about issues around confidentiality and about a feeling of not being taken seriously by staff. We also carried out a keyword analysis by comparing each age group with all of the others combined. This helped us to identify the different ways in which patients used language to construct their comments as legitimate. For example, people in their thirties were most likely to use 'you' to position their own experiences as being generalisable to the wider population, while people in their seventies used the term 'patients' to similar rhetorical effect.

Our analysis of sex and age in that corpus provided some interesting insights into differences but also similarities between the various sex and age-based groups making up our data. However, our necessary reliance on comments in which patients chose to self-report information about their sex and age meant that we were forced to work with small datasets, as the vast majority of patients did not explicitly reference these aspects of their identity in their comments. This meant that the samples we worked with represented a necessarily very small proportion of the comments overall. It could thus be argued that such patients were atypical in making explicit reference to their identities in this way and that they did so because they likely felt that such aspects of their identity somehow had a bearing on the care they received and/or were in some way relevant to the feedback they gave. Those findings thus need to be viewed through the perspective of a set of patients who self-declared such information and who, in this respect at least, were not typical of most patients providing feedback.

Yet while the restricted size of the samples we were able to work with through the self-referencing approach was certainly a limitation with respect to the generalisability of our findings, a potential advantage of this approach is that we could perhaps have more confidence that the particular identity categories we were investigating were indeed relevant to the evaluations being given, on the basis that the patients verbally referenced or 'topicalised' these aspects of their identity within their comments. In a sense, such an approach may be argued to narrow the interpretative leap that is involved when interpreting a feature of language use in terms of some aspect of the language user's identity. In this way, using language users' self-references to aspects of their identity as an entry point for studying identity in discourse may help to address the criticism of demographic metadata-based approaches that they assume that aspects of one's identity are the *cause* of some forms of language use, on the basis of statistical correlation. However, such an argument is difficult to falsify and depends to a great extent on our ontological assumptions. Regardless of where we stand on this debate, we are probably on safe ground to argue that the self-reference-based approach we adopted in Baker et al. (2019) represents at the very least a trade-off between, on the one hand, the confidence we can have in the generalisability of our findings and, on the other, the confidence we can have that a given identity category is relevant to a particular discourse or text (comment) or at a particular point within a text.

In this Element, we present analysis from a more recent project in which we again worked with the NHS in England, this time focussing on the analysis of patient feedback on cancer care services specifically. We consider the possible influence of patients' identities on how they evaluate their experiences of cancer care services, as well as the language they use in these evaluations. Like our previous analysis of healthcare feedback data, we focus on sex and age as identity variables. Our broad research question to ask the corpus is: how does patient age and sex relate to the nature of the feedback they give? Through this analysis, we want to explore several methodological issues that we (and others) have encountered when analysing identity in corpora. The first issue relates to the foregoing discussion; that is, how we go about identifying and examining aspects of identity in a corpus. So, in Sections 2 and 3 we compare two approaches to analysing identity in a corpus: one relying on the use of socio-demographic metadata annotations and the other using patients' references to their sex and age-related identities. Our analysis of patients' self-references to their sex identity in Section 2 and age in Section 3 then raises questions around how we should approach the analysis of such texts, particularly as taking this approach to the corpus usually results in us dealing with a smaller number of texts. Therefore, another methodological issue we explore in this Element involves a comparison of different ways of analysing large and small datasets. In Section 2 the same corpus-driven approach, keywords, is carried out on both small and large sub-corpora, while in Section 3 a small sub-corpus is analysed qualitatively via reading and categorising comments, while a larger sub-corpus is analysed through the corpus technique of collocation analysis. Therefore, as well as our research question based on sex and age, we have another question that links to methods: to what extent does an analysis of a small sample of comments containing 'on-record' reports of age or sex result in similar findings to analysis of a large corpus of comments where age and sex are tagged in the meta-data? And related to that, we ask, what kinds of findings do different methods of qualitative and quantitative analysis yield on these kinds of data?

We will describe our data and the methodological techniques we use in the next and final sub-section of this section.

1.5 Data and Methods

The data we analyse in this Element is a specialised corpus of written feedback on cancer care services provided by respondents to the England Cancer Patient Experience Survey (CPES). Responses were given both online and through pen-and-paper forms, with the latter subsequently being digitised to render them amenable to computational analysis. The CPES form allows patients to provide both quantitative and qualitative feedback. The quantitative component asks, 'Overall, how would you rate your care?', to which respondents can provide a score between zero and ten, where zero indicates that they definitely would not recommend a service and ten indicates that they definitely would. Respondents could then describe their experiences and explain the score they gave by providing qualitative feedback across three free-text boxes, which are preceded by the following questions: 'Was there anything particularly good about your NHS cancer care?', 'Was there anything that could have been improved?' and 'Any other comments?'. For the purposes of this Element, each 'comment' contains a respondent's comments on all three of these questions combined. The corpus comprises 214,340 comments (14,403,694 words), relating to hospitals across England, provided between 2015 and 2018. This data was made available to us by NHS England as part of a formal collaboration in which the organisation set us a series of questions to answer about the feedback, including answering questions about the influence of patient identity on the (language of the) feedback given.

The data was provided to us by NHS England's Insight and Feedback team in a spreadsheet in which each comment was accompanied by details about each respondent's care and certain socio-demographic characteristics, some that were obtained from patient records, others that were provided by patients themselves, as requested on the feedback form (we tagged each comment with meta-data about patient sex and age that had been derived via patient records).

Table 1 Breakdown of respondents in the corpus.

Age	%	Ethnicity	%
16–24	0.32	African	0.53
25–34	1.08	Arab	0.09
35–44	3.26	Bangladeshi	0.09
45–54	10.91	Caribbean	0.67
55–64	21.65	Chinese	0.22
65–74	36.08	English/Welsh/Scottish/ Northern Irish	87.09
75–84	22.36	Gypsy or Irish Traveller	0.02
85+	4.34	Indian	0.98
		Irish	1.03
Sex	**%**	Pakistani	0.34
Female	54.38	White and Asian	0.20
Male	45.62	White and Black African	0.08
No information given	<0.00	White and Black Caribbean	0.23
		Any other Asian background	0.45
Sexuality	**%**	Any other Black/African/ Caribbean background	0.08
Bisexual	0.27	Any other ethnic group	0.24
Gay or lesbian	0.73	Any other mixed background	0.16
Heterosexual	90.86	Any other White background	2.07
Other	0.32	No information available	5.43
Prefer not to say	1.87		
No answer	5.95	**Length of treatment**	**%**
		Less than 1 year	60.09
English first language	**%**	1–5 years	27.80
No	3.50	More than 5 years	7.65
Yes	92.40	Don't know/no answer	4.46
No information available	4.10		
		Year	**%**
		2015	24.57
		2016	25.16
		2017	24.40
		2018	25.87

The corpus was hosted and analysed on *CQPweb* (Hardie 2012). Table 1 gives a quantitative breakdown of the data respecting patients' characteristics. The information about age, sex and ethnicity were taken from patient records, information about sexuality, first language, length of treatment and year of survey were taken from the survey itself.

A limitation of this corpus relates to certain demographic (im)balances within it, which result in some demographic groups being underrepresented relative to others. For example, 87.09 per cent of the comments in our corpus were provided by patients identifying as White English/Welsh/Scottish/ Northern Irish. People from LGBTQ+ backgrounds make up just 1 per cent of respondents, while people who speak English as an additional language make up just 3.5 per cent. For this study we have gathered all available feedback in order to achieve as comprehensive coverage of patients as possible, though it is important to bear this skew in mind for our analysis.

The analysis reported over the next two sections focusses, as noted, on variability with respect to two of the socio-demographic characteristics represented in the metadata in Table 1: sex and age. For each analysis, we use the annotations to structure our data into sub-corpora respecting different sex and age groups. We also experiment with a different way of structuring the data, relying not on socio-demographic metadata tags but on respondents' explicit references to their sex or age in their comments. We will provide more specific information regarding the size and methods of down-sampling for these sub-corpora in the relevant sections. For now, we move on to briefly introduce the three corpus techniques we use in our analysis: keywords, collocation and concordance.

Keywords are words that occur with a significantly higher frequency in one corpus relative to another. The corpus that we compare our analysis corpus against is referred to as the reference corpus and this typically represents a norm or 'benchmark' for the type of language under investigation. Keywords are calculated based on statistical comparisons of the word frequency information for both corpora, with the frequency of each word in the analysis corpus compared against its equivalent in the reference corpus. If the difference between the relative frequencies is judged to be significant (according to a user-determined statistical measure), that word will be a keyword. The resulting keywords are then taken to be characteristic of the language in the corpus being analysed. Keywords are used in Section 2 to compare our sex-based samples of comments in order to ascertain forms of language use that are characteristic of male and female patients, relative to each other.

Collocation analysis is a word association measure that tells us how often two or more words occur alongside each other and whether this association is notable as a sizeable effect. Following Firth's (1957: 6) dictum that 'you shall know a word by the company it keeps', corpus linguists have sought insight into words' meanings and patterns of use by examining those words' patterns of co-occurrence, or 'collocation'. In Section 3 we use collocation analysis as a quantitative way into our age-tagged sub-corpora by analysing and categorising patients' comments based on the types of words that collocate frequently with their uses of certain forms of evaluative language in their comments.

The final technique we use in this Element, concordancing, provides a way of viewing corpus data that allows users to examine every occurrence of a word or phrase in context, thus allowing analysts to quickly scan for patterns of use. With the search word running down the centre of the screen and a few words of context displayed to the left and right, concordance output provides a useful means for spotting patterns that might be less obvious during more linear, left-to-right readings of the data. To help with such pattern-spotting, the concordance lines can also be sorted according to words immediately preceding or following the search-term. For a more contextualised view of the data, we can also access each original comment in its entirety by clicking the search word on a given concordance line. We use the concordance technique in both Sections 2 and 3 in order to formulate interpretations, respectively, of how the keywords and collocates are used in the corpus.

More specific detail, for example pertaining to the use of statistical measures and thresholds, is given in the relevant sections. Now we move onto the analysis, beginning in Section 2 with the study of patient sex.

2 Patient Sex

2.1 Introduction

This section reports our first case study, which examines the possible influence of patient sex and discourses around gender on feedback on cancer care services. We pursue this aim through two approaches, both based on the keywords technique. First, the male and female comments are compared by dividing up the comments in our corpus according to metadata relating to sex derived from patient records. We compare the two sets of comments with each other using the keywords technique, then qualitatively analyse random samples of 100 instances of each of the top thirty keywords from both sets of comments with the aim of interpreting the distinctive forms of language use in terms of the gendered discourses and other gender-based differences that characterise the feedback. In the second part of this section, we carry out the same analysis but from a different methodological perspective; specifically, we take a sample of comments in which patients go 'on record' about their sex by verbally referencing it in their comments. Rather than comparing these samples with each other directly, we compare both with the corpus as a whole, which we regard as a general corpus of cancer patient feedback. The resulting keywords are thus analysed both in terms of their differences and their similarities, with the former approached through keywords that emerge from both samples and the latter considered through keywords that are unique to either sample. As in the first part of the analysis, unique keywords are analysed in terms of sex-based differences (particularly focussing on those that articulate gendered discourses), while both unique and overlapping keywords are interpreted in terms of how comments featuring self-declarations of sex identity differ to patient feedback as a whole. As well as comparing feedback from men and women, then, through the analysis in this section we will compare two approaches to studying language and identity in corpora: one using corpus-internal indications of patient identity and the other using socio-demographic metadata.

2.2 Using Socio-Demographic Metadata

The first part of our analysis is, as noted, based on the use of socio-demographic metadata tags, which we used to create two subcorpora: one containing comments written by male patients and one containing comments written by female patients, with these categories derived from patient records (we do not include CPES responses where no comment was provided). We focus on male and female patients in this analysis because we do not have sufficient data to carry out keyword analysis on patients identifying as transgender or non-binary. In the corpus *transgender* occurred just five times, *trans* occurred just three times and there were no mentions of *non-binary* at all. It is worth pointing out that these surveys were conducted between 2015 and 2018 and more recently surveys have used a more inclusive question around sex, allowing for a wider range of options than just male or female.

There were 97,774 comments from male patients (5,720,898 words) and 116,564 comments from female patients (8,683,079 words). Comments from female patients are longer, on average, than comments from male patients (74.50 words versus 58.51 words, respectively). Out of this set of comments, 94,172 male patients (96.31 per cent) also answered question fifty-nine of the survey, which asked them 'Overall, how would you rate your care?' by circling a number on a scale of zero to ten, thus providing an overall quantitative rating for their care experiences, while 112,272 female patients answered this question (also 96.31 per cent). Table 2 shows the proportions, expressed as percentages, of male and female patients who gave each of the ratings between zero and ten, where zero is the most negative score and ten is the most positive. The final column of this table shows the difference in percentage between the two samples.

As Table 2 shows, both the male and female patients in our data were more likely to give the highest scores for the care they received with the

Table 2 Proportions of male and female patients who gave each of the ratings between zero and ten, expressed as percentages.

Rating	Male Patients (% of sample)	Female Patients (% of sample)	Percentage Difference (Male to Female)
0	0.15%	0.14%	−0.01%
1	0.22%	0.23%	+0.01%
2	0.27%	0.24%	−0.03%
3	0.44%	0.48%	+0.04%
4	0.69%	0.70%	+0.01%
5	1.62%	2.07%	+0.45%
6	2.22%	2.59%	+0.37%
7	6.47%	7.15%	+0.68%
8	18.68%	19.85%	+1.17%
9	29.74%	29.35%	−0.39%
10	39.50%	37.20%	−2.30%

overwhelming majority of both male and female patients giving scores of eight or above (87.92 per cent of male patients and 86.40 per cent of female patients for those who gave a rating) with the highest possible score of ten being the most popular for both groups. From the NHS's perspective, this is a positive outcome. The second point to note about Table 2 is that the proportions of male and female patients giving each rating are very similar. As the final column indicates, for nine of the eleven ratings the difference between each group is less than 1 per cent, while the largest difference is that the highest rating of ten was given by 2.30 per cent more male patients than female patients. However, even this difference is very small and generally the proportions for each score are similar. Overall, this suggests that there are no substantial differences, then, between male and female patients in terms of rates of satisfaction. Male and female patients are thus broadly comparable in terms of their satisfaction rates.

2.2.1 Male Patients' Keywords

We begin our analysis by using keywords to compare comments made by male patients with those made by female patients, as indicated by the socio-demographic metadata accompanying the feedback. Table 3 displays the top thirty keywords for the male patients' comments, ranked by log-likelihood (Dunning, 1993). Log-likelihood is a hypothesis-testing measure that identifies cases where there is confidence that a difference in a word's frequency exists between two corpora. It does not necessarily identify cases where there is

Table 3 Top thirty keywords for male patients' comments compared to female patients' comments, ranked by log-likelihood.

| Rank | Keyword | Target (Male Patient Comments) | | Reference (Female Patient Comments) | | Log Ratio | Log-likelihood |
		Freq.	Freq. PMW	Freq.	Freq. PMW		
1	class	4,969	868.61	2,693	310.15	1.49	1,968.30
2	bladder	2,611	456.42	882	101.58	2.17	1,767.59
3	treatment	46,228	8,080.88	56,738	6,534.46	0.31	1,147.26
4	good	25,776	4,505.77	30,364	3,496.99	0.37	890.62
5	hospital	39,990	6,990.44	50,339	5,797.49	0.27	778.59
6	NHS	12,360	2,160.59	13,449	1,548.91	0.48	708.22
7	first	13,534	2,365.81	15,159	1,745.85	0.44	655.35
8	no	23,674	4,138.33	28,795	3,316.29	0.32	633.62
9	by	20,851	3,644.86	25,114	2,892.35	0.33	605.51
10	condition	3,479	608.15	2,867	330.19	0.88	589.00
11	test	4,094	715.65	3,576	411.84	0.80	582.94
12	carried	2,382	416.39	1,784	205.46	1.02	515.86
13	blood	6,019	1,052.15	6,144	707.60	0.57	475.17
14	thanks	2,870	501.69	2,414	278.02	0.85	458.20
15	kidney	1,258	219.9	743	85.57	1.36	435.48
16	GP	15,544	2,717.17	18,896	2,176.23	0.32	417.45

17	bowel	2,348	410.44	1,957	225.39	0.86	384.88
18	endoscopy	846	147.88	443	51.02	1.54	352.03
19	)	18,719	3,272.17	23,687	2,728.01	0.26	344.01
20	yes	7,509	1,312.61	8,526	981.93	0.42	333.53
21	quality	1,520	265.7	1,136	130.83	1.02	330.79
22	problem	3,892	680.34	3,953	455.26	0.58	314.23
23	attention	2,518	440.16	2,297	264.54	0.73	310.56
24	period	1,336	233.54	989	113.90	1.04	297.30
25	general	3,452	603.43	3,491	402.06	0.59	284.14
26	months	6,853	1,197.94	7,891	908.80	0.40	277.48
27	removal	1,298	226.9	978	112.64	1.01	277.07
28	myeloma	1,306	228.3	989	113.90	1.00	275.43
29	professionalism	1,396	244.03	1,107	127.49	0.94	262.25
30	successful	854	149.28	551	63.46	1.23	253.04

a *strong* difference. Because it is based on confidence, it favours cases where there are a lot of data points, that is, higher-frequency words. This is useful when working with large corpora, in that low-frequency keywords can be unrepresentative or atypical. However, a limitation of log-likelihood is that, while the keywords produced tend to be highly frequent, the differences in the relative frequencies of the keywords between the target and the reference corpus can nevertheless be rather narrow for such high-frequency keywords. To guard against this unduly influencing our analysis, we also stipulated that keywords should have a positive log ratio score (Hardie, 2014). This effect-size measure indicates the strength of difference in the relative frequencies of keywords between the corpora, with keywords receiving higher log ratio scores being very much more frequent in the target corpus (for further discussion of keyword measures and the debates around them see Gabrielatos (2018) and Brookes and McEnery (2020)).

A further step we implemented here was to remove keywords that occurred less than fifty times per million words (PMW) in both corpora, which helped to filter out keywords that denoted proper nouns and sex-specific types of cancer, including the treatments associated with these. This did not lead to the removal of any other types of keywords. We should also note that *CQPweb* counts punctuation marks as tokens (or potential keywords), which is why we see the bracket as a keyword.

We then closely analysed the keywords in order to identify their main functions in the feedback and whether and how these might relate to the patients' sex identities. We used the *CQPweb* concordancer to access the uses of each keyword in their wider textual context, usually accessing entire comments to fully apprehend the keywords' functions. For keywords occurring less than 100 times, we analysed all cases. For keywords occurring more than 100 times, we randomly selected 100 cases for analysis.

Although the minimum frequency threshold successfully filtered out most of the keywords that were indicative of treatment that is particular or at least more prominent in the treatment of men relative to women, four of the remaining keywords – *bladder*, *bowel*, *kidney* and *myeloma* – indicate types of cancer that are more common in men (Cancer Research UK, 2021a; 2021b; 2022). However, such sex-based prevalence patterns do not explain the keyness of the more generic illness-referring nouns *condition* and *problem*, which were both key in the male comments. The marked frequency of these items in the male comments relative to the female ones indicates a pronounced focus in the former on the particular health issues that caused the male patients to visit a provider. Examining how these words were used by the male patients in their comments – based on random samples of 100 comments accessed through concordance – we observed that the keyness of these items resulted from the tendency for the male patients in our corpus to characterise their care in terms of processes, of which they, their bodies and their health problems are the objects. This trend helps to account for the keyness of several items in Table 3, including the verb *carried*, the nouns *blood* and *endoscopy*, the nominalising noun *removal* and *test*, which could be used as a noun or a verb. Note that for this and future examples we indicate the sex of the patient giving the comment as male (M) or female (F).

> My **condition** was discussed after a series of **blood tests** for diabetes, prostate **problems** and erectile dysfunction. (M)

This focus on the procedures involved in care and their rendering grammatically as processes also gives rise to the keyness of *by*, in cases where agency is ascribed to the person who performed the given procedure, including general practitioners (GP).

> These tests had been **carried out** for a long time to monitor a benign problem. Tests were **carried out by** the **GP**. (M)

The processes that the male patients evaluate in their comments are nominalised not only through reference to *removal*, but also in a more general sense in uses of the keywords *treatment* and *attention*, though the effect remains the same, that the focus of the male patients' feedback, relative to the female patients', is characteristically on the transactional aspects of service provision, rather than on the staff members themselves or the interpersonal relationships that patients have with staff.

As well as being presented as performing the procedures that the male patients undergo, staff working in healthcare are also indexed through uses of the keywords *hospital* and *NHS*, while *general* in turn helps to explain the keyness of *general* (i.e. 'General Hospital'). Both *NHS* and *hospital* could be used metonymically to refer to the staff they encountered, with the performance of a few staff members presented in terms of representing an entire hospital or even the NHS as a whole. Such metonymic constructions thus present the feedback – and the issues raised within it – as applying not just to a single staff member or team but rather to an entire site of care and even the healthcare system as a whole.

> Very happy with all aspects of treatment I have received from the **NHS**. Very impressed. (M)

> Systems let the **hospital** down – much waste of time and effort. Multiple files, shouldn't be too hard to integrate electronically across all Trust sites – money saver, stress saver and time saver! (M)

We would argue that, rhetorically, this kind of metonymic reference has the potential to present the male patients' experiences as applying not just to them or the individual staff members who treated them, but as being more generally applicable to staff comprising a hospital or even the entire NHS. Another feature of the male patients' comments, which is indicated in their pronounced use of *NHS*, is to comment on – or to relate their own experiences to – wider organisational issues within the NHS. Again, this may represent a rhetorical strategy used to generalise experiences and, in the case of complaints, to render these more pressing.

Another characteristic theme of the male patients' comments is time, as indicated in the keywords *months* and *period*. Analysis of these keywords in use reveals that they tend to be used to quantify the amount of time that the male patients have had to wait for something (usually a diagnosis or appointment for treatment). This theme – of waiting – is frequent in male and female patients' comments overall, while the more precise numbers given by the male patients to quantify the periods of their waits seems to be a gendered style feature that we previously observed in male patients' comments within more general NHS feedback (Baker et al., 2019).

> So I ended up waiting 6 **months** until they did surgery and remove what had to be removed, which is a very long wait if you keep in mind that this melanoma could spread in any moment and probably kill me. (M)

> The first thing to do on entering the department was always to look at the screen to whether there were any delays. These often changed mainly to extend the waiting **period** up to 1 hour. (M)

The male patients' focus on detail is also indicated in the keyness of the right-side bracket (*)*), which tends to be used to specify details such as the type of cancer that the male patients were treated for, the specific types of treatment or procedures they underwent and the ward or unit where they received that treatment.

> Biopsy results were too slow. Once received by medical staff, too long was taken in starting (further removal of skin cancer). Too many hospitals were involved ([name of hospital and ward]) in my opinion this resulted in months of inactivity and delay. (M)

Another set of keywords that indicates stylistic features characterising male patients' feedback is of those that are used to praise the objects of evaluation described earlier in this section, including the adjective keywords *good* and *first class*, the noun *professionalism* and *quality*, which could function as a positively valenced adjective or as a generic noun that received evaluation from other adjectives. Another keyword used to give praise – *successful* – is again indicative of the male patients' tendency to focus on the procedures they underwent in their feedback, as in 96 per cent of cases it was used by the male patients in reference to whether or not such procedures were a success.

> I had to go home and was called back the next week to have the operation, which was very **successful** again at [name of hospital]. (M)

The final group of keywords we want to consider for the male patients' comments is also reflective of style (*no, thanks, yes*). However, rather than necessarily reflecting how the male patients performed evaluation linguistically, the uses of these keywords are more reflective of how the male patients in our data interacted with the feedback form. In particular, these keywords were used in ways that suggested that the men interacted almost dialogically with the voice of the feedback form, by answering the prompt questions literally (*no, yes*) and performing the speech act of thanking service providers, who are assumed to be represented by the voice of the form.

> **Yes**. It was dealt with in a timely fashion and consideration was given by the consultant for the eventual cosmetic appearance of the site following removal of the lesion. (M)

> Just **thanks** for keeping me alive! (M)

Again, it is not entirely clear why the male patients are particularly likely to engage with the feedback form in this way. The relative frequency of these items, taken together, is 69,614 PMW for the male patients' comments and 64,730 PMW for the female patients' comments. Another factor here may be age. Table 4 gives a breakdown of how the numbers of comments and words for male and female patients are distributed across the age groups represented in the corpus.

Now, it is useful to compare these figures alongside the distribution of the keywords *no, thanks* and *yes* across the age groups for male and female patients. This is shown in Figures 1–3, which give the relative frequency (PMW) of the cumulative occurrences of these keywords for each sex group across the age categories.

As this graph shows, the relative frequency of each of these keywords is higher for male than female patients in all age groups, except for sixteen- to twenty-four-year-olds' use of *no*, which is fairly equal between the male and female samples. Furthermore, with a couple of exceptions, the use of these keywords generally increases in relative frequency for both male and female patients as we progress through the age categories before, in all but one case (female patients' use of *yes*), peaking with the oldest group (eighty-five plus). Referring back to Table 4, we see that patients in the two oldest age categories

Table 4 Breakdown of proportion of texts (all comments left by one person) and total words of comments from each age group for male and female patients.

Age Group	Male Patients		Female Patients	
	Texts	**Words**	**Texts**	**Words**
16–24	1.58%	2.07%	0.20%	0.22%
25–34	0.32%	0.39%	0.85%	1.14%
35–44	0.66%	0.92%	2.79%	3.63%
45–54	5.85%	7.25%	9.04%	11.20%
55–64	19.39%	22.09%	14.06%	15.62%
65–74	40.40%	40.96%	59.69%	58.69%
75–84	26.76%	22.42%	11.14%	8.06%
85+	5.05%	3.90%	2.23%	1.45%

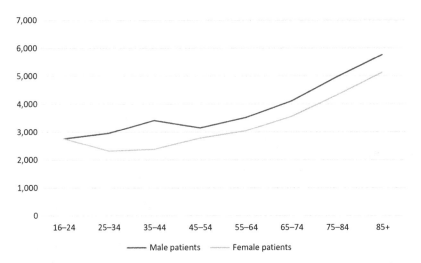

Figure 1 Distribution of frequency of *no* (PMW) for male and female patients across the age categories.

(seventy-five to eighty-four and eighty-five plus), who were most likely to use *no*, *yes* and *thanks*, made up much larger proportions of the feedback from men than women. Male patients aged seventy-five to eighty-four contributed 22.42 per cent of all the words in the male patients' comments overall (compared to just 8.06 per cent contributed by this age group in the female patients' comments), while those aged eighty-five plus contributed 3.9 per cent of all the words in the male patients' comments (compared to 1.45 per cent contributed by this age group in the female patients' comments). So, given that we know that

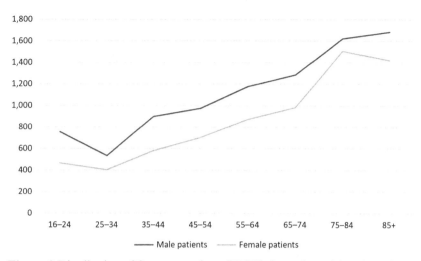

Figure 2 Distribution of frequency of *yes* (PMW) for male and female patients across the age categories.

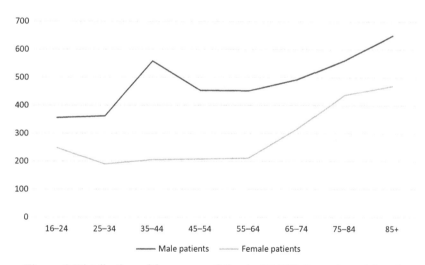

Figure 3 Distribution of frequency of *thanks* (PMW) for male and female patients across the age categories.

these keywords are most likely to be used by older patients, it may be the case that the keyness of these items is a product of the socio-demographic make-up of our corpus, with patients in this age group being more strongly represented in the male patients' feedback than the female patients'.

The general tendency for older patients to use *no*, *yes* and *thanks* more than younger groups suggests that the former are more likely to interact with the feedback form in a dialogic way, while younger groups are perhaps more likely to interpret the questions posed by the form as rhetorical, or at least as a prompt for a response that is not necessarily framed as a direct answer to the question posed. It may be the case that younger patients are more accustomed to the (synthetic) personalisation of such public discourse, rather than regarding it as an attempt by the organisation to establish personal dialogue. We explore the possible influence of patient age in the next section, so we will not focus on it further here. Now, we turn our attention to the female patients' comments.

2.2.3 Female Patients' Keywords

We obtained keywords for the female patients' comments by comparing them with the male patients' comments, which in this case served as our reference corpus. As before, we ranked our keywords using log-likelihood and removed those keywords that did not occur at least fifty times PMW in both corpora. As with our analysis of the male patients' comments in Section 2.2.2, this helped to filter out keywords that denoted sex-specific types of cancer and treatments. The resulting top thirty keywords are shown in Table 5.

While the male patients' comments were, as we have seen, focussed characteristically on procedural and transactional aspects of service, what are immediately striking in Table 5 are keywords that indicate a tendency for female patients to discursively situate themselves within their comments and the accounts they provide. This is reflected in the keyness of the first-person pronouns *I* and *me*. The relative overuse of such first-person forms in the female patients' comments also helps to explain the keyness of *had*, which tends to be applied to such first-person forms. Likewise, the keyword *did* tended to be used in negation (64 per cent of cases), including with the contraction *n't*, which was also key in the female patients' comments. Where *had* was used overwhelmingly in the construction of actions associated with the first-person (i.e. the patients themselves), *did* negated actions and attributes both of the patients and staff members (discussed later in this section).

The more personal focus in the female patients' comments also gives rise to a more characteristic focus in the female patients' comments on the emotional impacts that their experiences had on them, as indicated in uses of the keywords *felt* and *feel*. Examining the right-sided collocates (R1–R3) of *felt* and *feel*, we find that the most frequent feelings and emotions that the female patients describe include (frequency of co-occurrence in brackets): *safe* (813), [at] *ease* (698), *confident* (666), *cared* [for] (630) and *lucky* (617). The keywords from the female patients' comments discussed so far point to a greater focus on the interpersonal aspects of care, with the female patients

Table 5 Top thirty keywords for female patients' comments compared with male patients' comments, ranked by log-likelihood.

Rank	Keyword	Target (Female Patient Comments)		Reference (Male Patient Comments)		Log Ratio	Log-likelihood
		Freq.	Freq. PMW	Freq.	Freq. PMW		
1	*I*	302,785	34,871.45	172,520	30,157.33	0.21	2,426.7
2	*kind*	11,074	1,275.38	3,234	565.32	1.17	1,890.5
3	*felt*	13,101	1,508.83	4,221	737.85	1.03	1,821.45
4	*n't*	29,681	3,418.33	12,650	2,211.28	0.63	1,777.96
5	*amazing*	6,436	741.23	1,602	280.04	1.40	1,445.14
6	*feel*	16,105	1,854.8	6,214	1,086.24	0.77	1,378.82
7	*husband*	3,164	364.39	425	74.29	2.29	1,376.84
8	*she*	10,403	1,198.1	3,702	647.13	0.89	1,130.09
9	*so*	28,576	3,291.07	13,397	2,341.86	0.49	1,098.98
10	*lovely*	2,961	341.02	498	87.05	1.97	1,066.19
11	*oncologist*	7,901	909.95	2,675	467.6	0.96	976.39
12	*chemotherapy*	24,365	2,806.09	11,468	2,004.66	0.49	916.96
13	*me*	63,423	7,304.37	34,525	6,035.14	0.28	834.39
14	*they*	39,214	4,516.24	20,323	3,552.56	0.35	792.50
15	*had*	73,119	8,421.04	40,891	7,147.94	0.24	720.46
16	*radiotherapy*	12,972	1,493.97	5,642	986.25	0.60	712.87

Table 5 (cont.)

Rank	Keyword	Target (Female Patient Comments)		Reference (Male Patient Comments)		Log Ratio	Log-likelihood
		Freq.	Freq. PMW	Freq.	Freq. PMW		
17	*her*	6,637	764.38	2,441	426.70	0.84	657.05
18	*wonderful*	7,106	818.39	2,684	469.18	0.80	649.85
19	*did*	21,234	2,445.50	10,382	1,814.82	0.43	641.20
20	*you*	31,028	3,573.46	16,132	2,819.95	0.34	611.00
21	*nurse*	20,478	2,358.43	10,145	1,773.39	0.41	568.95
22	*unit*	11,739	1,351.97	5,266	920.52	0.55	561.76
23	*when*	31,967	3,681.61	16,882	2,951.05	0.32	553.81
24	*wait*	10,315	1,187.97	4,526	791.17	0.59	545.51
25	*supportive*	4,998	575.61	1,822	318.49	0.85	507.46
26	*lump*	2,183	251.41	532	93.00	1.43	505.89
27	*chemo*	6,056	697.46	2,368	413.94	0.75	496.03
28	*everyone*	9,969	1,148.12	4,476	782.43	0.55	474.99
29	*caring*	18,756	2,160.11	9,529	1,665.72	0.37	438.86
30	*busy*	4,188	482.33	1,518	265.35	0.86	432.14

foregrounding how they were made to feel during an episode of treatment, which could be contrasted with the more procedural focus of the male patients' feedback examined in Section 2.2.2. Other keywords in the female patients' comments provide further evidence for this focus on interpersonal aspects of care, as staff members are evaluated as *kind*, *lovely*, *supportive* and *caring*. Staff receive particular praise from female patients when they perform well at these aspects of their roles when they are also perceived to be *busy*.

Staff were **lovely**, but all too **busy**. (F)

The keyness of other evaluation words in Table 5 is less easily explained but may be interpreted as evidence of a gendered style, with the female patients being more likely to evaluate staff as *amazing* or *wonderful* and being more likely to use the intensifier *so*. Examining 100 randomly selected uses of each of these keywords, we again find that they tend to be used in reference to staff members' interpersonal skills. This finding echoes our previous analysis of general patient feedback, which found that, in both their positive and negative comments, female patients foregrounded staff interpersonal skills more than male patients did.

Given the pronounced focus on interpersonal skills in the female patients' comments, it is perhaps unsurprising to find keywords that indicate a stronger focus on individuals (*she*, *oncologist*, *her*, *nurse*), including the roles and experiences of relatives (*husband*), units and smaller teams of staff (*they*, *unit*). Meanwhile, *chemotherapy*, *radiotherapy* and *chemo*, while referring ostensibly to types of treatment, were also used to refer to teams of staff (including metonymically through references to specific wards).

The nurses in the **chemo** ward were absolutely fantastic at [name] Unit. (F)

This represents another difference between the male and female patients' comments, since, as we have seen, the male patients tended to present their evaluations as pertaining to entire hospitals and even the healthcare system as a whole in their comments, rather than framing these in terms of the individuals involved in the provision of care. Even the more generalising *everyone*, which may ostensibly refer to all staff working within a provider, tends to be limited to a particular provider, unit, ward or team.

Almost without exception, every member of staff I interacted with was tremendously caring, nothing is too much trouble to help a patient. This includes **everyone** from cleaners and security staff to the CEO. (F)

As well as referring to teams of staff, the keyword *everyone* is also used to refer to other patients who attend a particular provider. Such uses could be interpreted as a rhetorical strategy whereby the women in our data render their experiences as more generalisable (as we saw with some of the male patients' keywords earlier). Another strategy that the female patients characteristically draw on to this end is the use of the general *you*.

> **Everyone** is looked after in the same wonderful way. (F)

> All staff in the cancer care unit are friendly, caring and helpful. They all welcome **you** and take care of **you** as if **you** are a part of the family. (F)

We are getting a sense, then, of some differences between the male and female comments; both male and female patients seem to deploy rhetorical strategies to make their feedback appear to be more generalisable; they just go about it differently. Another shared concern for male and female patients is the theme of waiting. In Section 2.2.2, we saw how use of the keywords *months* and *period* in the male patients' comments indicated a focus on waits, which tended to be quantified in rather precise terms. The female patients in our data also focused on waits, as indicated in the final keyword we consider here – *wait*. However, when female patients described and evaluated waits, they did so in much less precise terms; analysis of 100 cases of the keyword *wait* revealed that women specified the length of their waits in just 15 per cent of cases. This may be why we see words such as *months* and *period* as key for the men's comments relative to the women's, even if both groups focus on the theme of waiting in their feedback.

> Sometimes I have a long **wait** on surgery day but I don't think this can be helped. (F)

Having utilised socio-demographic metadata to compare the male and female patients' feedback, we now attempt to carry out a similar analysis but this time without the help of such metadata, instead deriving samples from our corpus based on patients' explicit mentions of their sex or gender (e.g. being male or female or a man or a woman) in their comments.

2.3 Using Patient Mentions of Sex

Section 2.2 was based on comparing sub-corpora of comments organised using metadata tags relating to patients' sex. In this section, we demonstrate a different approach by analysing comments in which patients verbally reference their sex identity. We are interested not only in comparing the comments written by male and female patients when they make these aspects of their identity marked but, by comparing the findings from this section to those reported in Section 2.2, we are also interested in considering the kinds of insights we get when we study cases where patients' sex is linguistically marked compared to cases where it is not.

The first step in this analysis involved collecting texts for our samples of comments from male and female patients. To obtain comments in which patients linguistically marked their identity, we searched for use of *man* and *woman* and then extracted 100 comments in which patients self-identified as men and 100 comments in which patients self-identified as women. We manually checked the results to ensure that patients were indeed referencing their own sex identity (e.g. 'As a 25-year old *man*', 'I am an intelligent *woman*') and excluded cases where they were referencing another person (e.g. 'the doctor was a nice *man*', 'a *woman* in the next bed'). This gave us two sub-corpora: one containing 100 comments written by male patients (14,067 words) and the other containing 100 comments written by female patients (20,219 words). We should note that we decided to look at just 100 comments for male and female patients each because our data contained exactly 100 comments in which male patients referenced their sex in this way. For female patients, we had slightly more (134), but we focused on just 100 of these as wanted to balance the number of comments in our corpora.

For this analysis, we decided to adopt a slightly different approach to obtaining keywords than taken in Section 2.2. As a reminder, we compared the two sub-corpora (respectively containing the male and female patients' comments) against each other directly, with either corpus serving as the 'reference' for the other. This approach was, as we have seen, productive for studying differences between either set of comments. However, one issue with this is that the direct comparison leads to a focus on differences between the two sub-corpora at the expense of possible similarities. For the analysis of the samples reported in this section, we adopted a different approach; we compared both samples separately against the remainder of the comments in our corpus, which serve here as a reference corpus representing general feedback on NHS cancer care services. These comparisons thus yielded two sets of keywords, one for the sample of male patients who self-referenced their sex identity and one for the sample of female patients who self-referenced their sex identity.

An advantage of this approach is that it allows us to consider not only differences but also similarities between the samples, as indicated in keywords that are shared by both samples. Such shared keywords can be viewed as indicating what is linguistically distinctive about comments provided by patients who self-reference their sex identity relative to those who do not. Meanwhile, the distinct keywords – which do *not* overlap – can be interpreted as indicating potential sex-related differences (i.e. what is distinctive about when male or female patients reference their sex in their feedback).

A disadvantage of this approach is that, while distinct keywords may indicate differences between the two samples, these differences are not necessarily statistically significant or at least as strong as the differences that are shown in keywords obtained by comparing two corpora directly against each other. This is important to bear in mind.

Since, as will be evident, the keywords obtained through the procedure described yielded a mixture of distinct but also overlapping keywords between the two samples, this section of the analysis will be presented differently to the previous one. Rather than present and analyse the men's and women's keywords separately, we will present both sets of keywords together, to enable the subsequent analysis to comment on both similarities and differences.

We began by comparing our sample of 100 male patients' comments against the rest of the corpus (including both male and female comments, together). As before, we combined log-likelihood with log ratio to measure and rank the keywords. Again, we stipulated that keywords should receive a positive log ratio score. Regarding log-likelihood, since the scores assigned to these keywords were much lower than those analysed in Section 2.2 (due to their considerably lower frequencies), it was necessary to impose a minimum threshold of 15.13 (which indicates a 99.99 per cent likelihood that keywords are in fact key and have not arisen as such due to a sampling error). This gave fifteen keywords, which are displayed in Table 6.

We then repeated the procedure for the sample of female patients' comments, comparing this against the remainder of the corpus and measuring and ranking keywords in the same way. This produced nineteen keywords, given in Table 7.

Having obtained our sets of keywords, we then undertook a close analysis of them in order to identify their main functions in the feedback and whether and how these might relate to the patients' self-referenced sex identities. This analysis proceeded in the same way as the analysis of keywords in Section 2.2; namely, we used the CQPweb concordancer to access the use of each keyword in their wider textual context, usually accessing entire comments to fully apprehend the keywords' functions. For keywords occurring less than 100 times, we analysed all cases. For keywords occurring more than 100 times, we randomly selected 100 cases for analysis.

First, we want to note that, like the keyword comparison of patient sex across the whole corpus reported in the first half of this section, the comparison of the sex-based samples has also yielded keywords that gesture towards types of cancer and their associated treatments that are either exclusive to, or at least particularly common to, either men or women. For example, from the male patients' sample we get the keyword *prostate*, while in the female patients' sample there is *ovarian*. Also, concerns around hair loss resulting from cancer

Table 6 Keywords for the sample of male patients' comments compared to the rest of the corpus, ranked by log-likelihood.

Rank	Keyword	Target (Male Patient Sample)		Reference (Remainder of the Corpus)		Log Ratio	Log-likelihood
		Freq.	Freq. PMW	Freq.	Freq. PMW		
1	man	114	7,351.52	813	56.50	7.02	869.52
2	old	24	1,547.69	1,581	109.88	3.82	82.09
3	a	337	21,732.12	210,295	14,615.81	0.57	47.40
4	said	32	2,063.58	8,142	565.88	1.87	36.32
5	I	642	41,400.66	474,670	32,990.26	0.33	31.84
6	that	149	9,608.56	87,566	6,085.96	0.66	27.00
7	lucky	17	1,096.28	3,739	259.87	2.08	22.97
8	prostate	19	1,225.25	4,739	329.37	1.90	22.11
9	am	63	4,062.68	31,706	2,203.61	0.88	19.45
10	life	22	1,418.71	6,836	475.11	1.58	18.85
11	we	35	2,257.05	14,284	992.76	1.18	18.28
12	young	8	515.90	1,040	72.28	2.84	17.64
13	now	29	1,870.12	11,573	804.34	1.22	15.88
14	"	22	1,418.71	7,677	533.56	1.41	15.56
15	sick	8	515.90	1,243	86.39	2.58	15.24

Table 7 Keywords for the sample of female patients' comments compared to the rest of the corpus, ranked by log-likelihood.

| Rank | Keyword | Target (Female Patient Sample) | | Reference (Remainder of the Corpus) | | Log Ratio | Log-likelihood |
		Freq.	Freq. PMW	Freq.	Freq. PMW		
1	*age*	23	1,031.99	1,650	114.73	3.17	59.93
2	*old*	20	897.38	1,585	110.21	3.03	48.62
3	*women*	15	673.04	821	57.09	3.56	46.34
4	*younger*	10	448.69	250	17.38	4.69	45.43
5	*hair*	12	538.43	522	36.30	3.89	42.11
6	*wig*	10	448.69	357	24.82	4.18	38.75
7	*intelligent*	7	314.08	139	9.67	5.02	34.84
8	*children*	10	448.69	559	38.87	3.53	30.51
9	*should*	62	2,781.89	19,414	1,349.94	1.04	25.83
10	*fertility*	5	224.35	113	7.86	4.84	23.67
11	*me*	211	9,467.40	97,738	6,796.14	0.48	20.95
12	*said*	32	1,435.81	8,142	566.15	1.34	20.77
13	*!*	78	3,499.80	29,088	2,022.61	0.79	19.70
14	*this*	136	6,102.21	58,947	4,098.83	0.57	19.00
15	*ovarian*	8	358.95	677	47.07	2.93	18.53
16	*be*	162	7,268.81	73,758	5,128.71	0.50	17.67
17	*that*	187	8,390.54	87,528	6,086.19	0.46	17.46
18	*age*	23	1,031.99	1,650	114.73	3.17	59.93
19	*old*	20	897.38	1,585	110.21	3.03	48.62

treatment are more prevalent in the female patients' feedback, which results in the keyness of *hair* and *wig* in those comments. Likewise, although cancer can affect fertility in both male and female patients, the words *fertility* and *children* are tellingly key in the female sample but not the male sample. These keywords thus provide further evidence for the sense in which male and female patients' comments are each more useful for looking at particular issues. This enhances our understanding of the content of the patients' comments, then, which may be a useful insight from the perspective of feedback monitors.

Other keywords across Tables 6 and 7 are more revealing in terms of similarities and differences in the linguistic style in which male and female patients provide feedback. A striking similarity between both lists is the keyness of the quotative *said*, as well as in the case of the male patients' comments, the speech mark ("). These keywords indicate a tendency for commenters in both samples to quote others in their feedback relatively more often than we would find in our general corpus of comments. This also helps to explain the keyness of *that*, which tends in both samples to be used to frame quotations, as in the examples below.

> He said **that** an 80 year old man like me was exposed to bacterial and viral infections, far more in hospital than I was in my own home! (M)

> My otherwise very supportive oncologists said **that** I was the only woman ever to have mentioned this as an issue. I am not the only woman! (F)

The use of quotations is not itself likely to be a gendered feature, as it was reflected in keywords in both the male and female patients' samples. Moreover, and as these examples attest, quotatives tended to be used to support negative evaluations, with patients often describing being given inconsistent or inaccurate advice or expressing consternation at the perceived rudeness that they inferred from a staff member's speech or communication style. This use of quoted speech is a general feature of – particularly negative – healthcare feedback, as observed in Baker et al. (2019). In that study, we linked the use of quotatives in (particularly negative) feedback to findings from research on focus groups, which found that reported speech was used by discourse participants expressing contentious sentiments, such as criticisms (Myers, 1999). Couper-Kuhlen (2007: 82) argues that reported speech can 'heighten [the] evidentiality' of a claim. Thus, we have argued, it may be the case that patients utilise reported speech to strengthen the credibility of their complaints by citing that reported speech as a form of evidence.

Although both the male and female samples exhibited a pronounced use of quotatives, close analysis of this feature in use also revealed some subtle differences between the samples that may gesture towards gender-based style differences and which also help to explain why quotative use was more frequent in these samples relative to the corpus of comments in general. In both samples, men and women could frame a particular comment or communicative style attributed to a staff member as being inappropriate given the patient's sex, along with other aspects of their identity. One such aspect, as indicated in both sets of keywords, is age.

Age-related words can be found in both sets of keywords. For the male patients' comments, these include *old* and *young*, while for the female patients' comments they include *age*, *old* and *younger*. Both male and female patients could use the keyword *old* to describe their age straightforwardly (e.g., 'As a 68 year old man ', 'I am a 72 year old woman'). Such patterns help to explain the keyness of *old* in both samples. Yet further patterns in the use of the age-related keywords are more revealing regarding how patients referenced their identities in their comments, including to evaluative effect. Both male and female patients referenced their age in conjunction with their sex in order to construct an intersectional identity (Crenshaw, 1993) in their comments. The concept of intersectionality advocates a view of identity as a fluid interaction between various aspects (e.g. sex, age, ethnicity, social class, sexuality, and so on). As Baker (2008: 11–12) puts it,

> [a]lthough we often talk about identity in the singular, it could be said that we have identities made up of many different and interacting components. . . . So individuals could be said to hold a sex identity, a gender identity and a sexual identity, as well as an ethnic identity, a national identity, a social class identity, an age identity, a religious identity, a work identity, a physical appearance or body identity etc. It is the sum of these identities that makes us who we are.

The referencing of sex and age together is, of course, not likely to be a feature specific to the genre of patient feedback. However, when it does occur in these comments, we could argue that such occurrences in this context signal that patients view the intersection of their sex and age identities to be in some way relevant such as in the examples in which patients straightforwardly mention their sex and age together imply that these aspects of their identity are relevant to their healthcare experiences or their evaluations of these. Yet there is also evidence of such intersectional identities being constructed to more explicitly evaluative effect, and such evaluations seemed to draw on wider sets of discourse around both sex and age. Both male and female patients could reference their age in order to construct themselves as having particular health-care requirements. If these requirements were met, this resulted in positive evaluation. However, if these requirements were judged not to have been met, the resulting evaluation was negative.

An **old** man, I am fortunate to be looked after and I dare to say loved by so many dedicated and caring professionals. (M)

Future impacts of chemotherapy, such as infertility, were shrugged off as irrelevant and I felt like a bit of a lost cause, which is pretty disheartening for a 27-year-**old** woman. (F)

Yet, as well as being drawn upon in support or justification of an evaluation of healthcare services, discourses around the intersection of gender and age – and the stereotypes inherent within these – could also be rejected by patients. In such cases, the discourses themselves were the target of the negative evaluation, along with the staff members who were presented as behaving in a way that was congruous with the harmful or inaccurate discourse. For example, one man complained about being treated like a 'grumpy old man', while another complained of being treated like a 'dirty old man'.

The ward nursing staff were very poor as far as myself was concerned. I was treated as a dirty **old** man (not clean) in spite of being told about my physical state. (M)

Both male and female patients drew on the intersection of age and sex to frame descriptions of experiences in which they felt patronised by staff members.

I was treated as if I was a silly **old** man, ordered to get into bed and told to take tablets that I did not recognise and did not know what they were for. (M)

A little compassion should be used when scan results show growth of cancer. If the patient has an unusual cancer, the consultant should make sure they have some knowledge concerning this cancer. A patient should be listened to not treated as a silly **old** woman. This sentence should be never said to a patient 'it's not that I don't believe you, I've just not heard that before'! (F)

The particular prominence of this discourse in the female patients' comments is also indicated by the keyness of *intelligent* in the female comments, where patients constructed themselves as *intelligent*. In all cases, the female patients in our sample provided positive feedback for staff who treated them like intelligent women. However, the notability or 'tellability' (Polanyi, 1979) of this aspect may suggest that some of the female patients in our sample expected that they may not have been treated as intelligent. Indeed, they may have expected to be patronised as in the comments quoted. Thus, the uses of *intelligent* in these comments may be the product of a wider societal discourse that women are not regarded or treated as being as intelligent as men.

I was always treated with respect and compassion. I was treated as an **intelligent**, educated woman. (F)

Just as the male and female patients referenced their age as older, the keywords in both tables also suggest that these patients constructed themselves in terms of their youth. In the male patients' comments, the keyword *young* is used by them to construct themselves as socially and sexually active, with these aspects of their identity being linked to both their age and gender and used as a warrant for positive or negative feedback. The following example also demonstrates how concerns around *prostate* cancer (another of the male patients' keywords) could be framed in terms of its potential impact on the male patients' lifestyles.

> My operation was arranged and carried out just about as quickly and effi-ciently as it could have been. Following the removal of my prostate, more emphasis could have been placed on penile rehabilitation. It was only by asking for further treatment that it was offered. As a relatively **young** man, my sexual health is of the utmost importance to me. Recovery may have been delayed. Thank you ever so much to the NHS! (M)

Where the adjective *young* is key in the male patients' comments, the related comparative form *younger* is key in the female patients' comments. In contrast to the male patients' comments, in which the commenters tended to use *young* in reference to themselves, the female patients tended to use *younger* in a general and hypothetical sense to refer either to younger female patients in general or to hypothetical others. Such comments typically described how particular aspects of service would not be suitable for younger (female) patients, and/or made recommendations about how services could be improved for *younger* others.

> The system is designed for a middle-aged woman going through a diagnosis, not a **younger** woman. (F)

> Massive room for improvement needed to support a **younger** woman going through a cancer diagnosis. My life turned upside down overnight being diagnosed aged 30. The clinics can be isolating when you are there with people twice your age. Could it be looked at that a clinic for **younger** women was scheduled both for appointments and potentially at chemotherapy? (F)

Similarly, the other age-related keyword in the women's comments, *age*, could be used to refer to a general, hypothetical other. Again, such constructions typically described whether an aspect of service would or would not be suitable for female patients of a particular age and, in the case of the latter, to make recommendations for improvements.

This focus on relating experiences to female patients more widely, and to issuing recommendations on the basis of those experiences, also helps to account for the keyness of certain grammatical items in the female patients' sample, too; namely, *this*, *be* and *should*. Specifically, *this* is used to deictically refer to the experience or circumstances described in the comment. Meanwhile, *be* tends to be used as a copula verb to construct hypothetical scenarios in which the circumstances denoted by *this* (among other forms of deictic reference) apply to other patients and other women, as the following example demonstrates. The modal verb keyword *should*, meanwhile, supports the issuing of recommendations by describing how things *should* be done in the future and for other patients (including other female patients).

> All patients in UK **should** have, along with their details, an online family tree with all their family members, 2 or 3 generations, with type of major disease they all suffered from and age (cancer, heart, stroke). **This** could **be** accessed directly by the patient to update it, nurses, doctors and then children could use it in turn when 18. (F)

So where the keywords from the female patients' sample indicate an orientation in these comments to others, and the possible future experiences of those hypothetical others, we do not get a sense of this type of focus from the male patients' sample. Rather, the keywords from these comments suggest a more characteristic focus on the self and one's own experiences. This was indicated in use of the keyword *young* we saw earlier, where in contrast to the female patients' relational use of *younger* (which referred, in hypothetical and relational terms, to other women), the adjective keyword *young* was used by the men to refer exclusively to themselves and their own experiences.

Returning to the male patients, and this sense in which they focussed more than the female patients on their own experiences, and less on those of (even hypothetical) others, also manifests in a discourse of exceptionalism in the male patients' comments, which is realised through uses of the keyword *lucky*. The male patients in our sample used this word in wider positive evaluative passages in which they either described themselves as *lucky* for having been treated by a highly skilled practitioner or team or describe exchanges with staff in which they are told they are *lucky* to be alive, such was the severity of their condition.

> I am a very **lucky** man to get such treatment. (M)

> I am a very **lucky** man thanks to the expertise and staff care from all the staff in [name of hospital], I have survived cancer. (M)

In either case, what is telling here is that the male commenters imply, through their use of *lucky*, that their experiences are somehow exceptional or even unique, either in terms of the high standards of care they received or the severity of their cancer. Cases of the latter also help to explain the keyness of *sick* in the male patients' sample, in particular in comments where the men describe how staff informed them that they were (very) *sick* men.

> When I saw the consultant after the diagnostic tests (a colorectal consultant), I was told that I was a very **sick** man. (M)

Another keyword that indicates the male patients' focus on their own experiences is the temporal adverb *now*. Earlier, we saw how one of the ways in which the female patients in our sample addressed the experiences of others was through reference to, and recommendations regarding, care provided to hypothetical others both now and in the future. Rather than having this orientation to the future, the male patients' comments can be better characterised by a focus on the past as well as the present. Descriptions of the past again adopt a personal perspective and even take on an almost personal, autobiographical tone, with the male patients relaying their previous experiences and the different forms of treatment that have brought them to the present (i.e. *now*).

> In the early days of treatment for bladder cancer the hospital was under private enterprise and service and efficiency was excellent and second to none, but **now** it is back to normal. Parking was free to blue badge holders but **now** we have to pay a minimum 2.90 each time we are called for consultation or treatment (M)

Thus, while *now* ostensibly refers to the present, the function of its use in the male patients' comments is to draw comparisons with their experiences in the past or to locate the present within a series of events stretching back into their past. A similar trend can also be observed in the male patients' use of the keyword *life*, which the male patients in the sample used either to thank staff for saving or improving their lives or to evaluate an experience as being the worst of their life.

> These 5 days were the worst 5 days of my entire **life**. No sleep. No rest! Have separate wards for dementia patients. (M)

Thus, use of these keywords *now* and *life* reveal how some of the male patients in our sample contextualise their experiences by comparing these to their own previous experiences, rather than those of (hypothetical or imagined) others, in the way that the patients in our female sample did.

The male patients' more restricted focus on themselves and their own, personal experiences also manifested through the way the men in our sample discursively positioned themselves within their comments. In particular, amongst the male keywords we find the first-person pronoun *I*, along with the associated form *am*. In the male patients' comments, *I* tends to function as a subject pronoun and can be used to position the male patients as the 'doers' of actions, including perceptual and cognitive processes but also material processes such as undergoing operations.

> If the cancer had been diagnosed earlier (by my GP) the neurosurgical operation **I** underwent would probably not have been necessary (M)

The clauses in which the male patients used *I* performed a range of functions, including describing processes in which the male patients could have just as easily been positioned as the object, such as undergoing operations, as the example here attests. By contrast, among the female patients' keywords we find the equivalent first-person form to be the object pronoun *me*, which was used consistently by the female patients in our sample to construct themselves as the recipients of actions or processes, or in other words to position themselves as the 'done to'.

> I felt emotionally traumatised by this woman who performed a sentinel node biopsy on **me**. (F)

As the previous two examples show, differing preferences regarding the use of self-referring pronominals can provide quite distinct representations of the same event (in this case, undergoing an operation). Specifically, the male patients' preference for *I* indicates their tendency to ascribe agency to themselves and to foreground themselves and their role within the clause (tending to occur at the beginning of the sentence), with the possibility that the staff member(s) involved in carrying out the procedure is elided from the discourse altogether. On the other hand, the preference for *me* in the female patients' sample reflects their tendency to construe themselves in more passive roles, as the recipients of processes like operations, where the focus of the clause is arguably the staff member(s) involved who are not only mentioned in the clause but also tend to be positioned in the most prominent, clause-initial position. On one hand, these differences between the male and female comments can, as noted, be read as further manifestations of the tendency for the former to focus on themselves and their experiences and the latter to address more explicitly how others are involved in or otherwise might be affected by their experiences. What we see here is that the female patients' focus on others includes not only other patients but also extends to the staff members involved in their care, which is consistent with our findings on the general comparison of male and female patients' comments in the whole corpus reported in the first half of this section. On the other hand, it is also possible that the tendency for the male and female patients to construct themselves, respectively, as active and passive participants in discourse may represent evidence of a general discourse of male agentivity and female passivity (Sunderland, 2004) permeating into men's and women's everyday language use.

2.4 Conclusions

In this section we have applied two approaches to study the influence of gender and patients' sex identity on their comments. In the first half, we used the socio-demographic metadata accompanying the feedback to compare comments from male and female patients using the keywords approach. Some of the keywords produced through this comparison indicated differences in the thematic content of the comments and what was focussed on or foregrounded within them. For example, the male patients' comments focussed on transactional aspects of care, such as operations, whereas female patients' comments focussed more often on the individuals who performed those operations, as well as on the interpersonal relationships that the female patients established with staff members.

There were also some similarities in thematic content in terms of what male and female patients foregrounded from their experience. However, there were differences in the style in which such themes were described and evaluated. Male patients focus on detail in terms of waits, such as the duration of waits, where the female patients talked about waits in vaguer terms.

Towards the end of the first half of our analysis, we noted a further stylistic characteristic of male patients' comments, with keywords suggesting that the male patients were more likely than the female ones to engage in an almost dialogic way with the 'voice' of the feedback form. For example, the male patients answered the rhetorical questions that framed the free text boxes in literal terms and directed thanks to the voice of the feedback form for the quality of care provided. At that point, it was useful to draw on the wider metadata, which allowed us to see that the language use associated with this style was associated with older patients more than younger patients. Since the male patients in our corpus are, on average, older than the female patients, we concluded that this feature was likely to derive from age differences between the two groups as represented in our data, rather than being to do with sex per se.

In the second half of the section, we adopted a different approach in which we disregarded the metadata available to us and instead based our analysis on samples of comments in which patients went on record about their sex or gender identity in the comments themselves. Some of the differences identified in the first half of the analysis were echoed, or at least consistent with, findings from the second part of the analysis. It is worth bearing in mind that the differences we identified between the male and female patients' samples in the second part of our analysis were not necessarily statistically significant relative to each other, as we did not compare these samples against each other directly. Rather, we based this analysis on keywords generated by comparing each sample to the same reference corpus, that is to say our corpus of NHS cancer comments as a whole.

Taken together, then, the two approaches to keyword analysis used in this section have revealed a set of complementary insights into the influence of sex identity and gendered discourses on the patient comments in our corpus. At this point, we want to reflect on either approach in terms of their advantages and disadvantages, as well as what each has added or can supplement in terms of the other. The first approach, which was based on socio-demographic metadata, was advantageous in as much as it allowed us to base our findings on a much larger dataset. This not only means that we can have greater confidence in the trends we identified, but it also allowed us to compare our sex-based subsets of the corpus directly, which meant that the differences identified through keyword comparison did in fact represent statistically significant differences in the language used by the male and female patients in our data. Of course, assembling a corpus of this size with reliable metadata is no mean feat, and so the benefits of a larger corpus and the increased optionality of using statistical measures is a relative argument and will only apply to the extent that researchers are able to build such a large corpus and then reliably annotate it for such socio-demographic information. However, the argument in favour of approaches that facilitate corpora that are larger and likely to be more representative is nevertheless a compelling one, particularly when we consider how much smaller the corpora analysed in the second half of the section were and the fact that this reduces the level of confidence we can have in the generalisability of the patterns we observed in those samples.

Another advantage of the reliable metadata we used in the first half of this section is that it also allowed us to draw on other metadata tags in order to interpret the patterns we found. In particular, our finding that male patients engaged with the feedback form in a relatively more dialogic way than the female patients could only really be interpreted in view of the generally older age of the male patients relative to the female patients. This was a supplementary perspective that was only possible by being able to draw on this extra socio-demographic information. In other words, without being able to draw on the age-related metadata in addition to the sex-related metadata, we simply would not have arrived at that interpretation. We utilise these age-related tags more extensively in Section 3, but for now it is worth noting that an advantage of having this diverse socio-demographic metadata, and of marking it up in our corpus, is that our analysis could come closer to the influence of intersectional identity on the discourse in our corpus.

3 Patient Age

3.1 Introduction

The research question we consider in this section concerns how patient age relates to positive and negative feedback. Age is a central feature in healthcare contexts, as many health conditions are more likely to appear at certain points in a person's life-span. This is true for cancer – those aged between zero and fourteen and fifteen and twenty-four each account for less than 1 per cent of new cancer cases, while people aged twenty-five to forty-nine account for 9 per cent. The fifty to seventy-four group make up more than half of new cases (54 per cent), while people aged seventy-five or above account for 36 per cent (Cancer Research, 2021c). Additionally, different types of cancer affect different age groups to varying extents. For males under fourteen, brain cancer and leukaemias account for 57 per cent of cancers, while for those aged fifty to seventy-four, prostate and lung cancer are most common, accounting for 43 per cent of cases. For females under fourteen, it is also brain cancer and leukaemias that make up 57 per cent of cancers, whereas breast cancer and lung cancer account for 47 per cent of cancers for women aged fifty to seventy-four (Cancer Research, 2021c).

We adopt a similar approach to identifying age in the first half of this section, mindful of both its advantages and disadvantages. In keeping with Section 2, we carry out two forms of analysis. First, a qualitative analysis based on reading samples of feedback and categorising positive and negative comments. Second, an analysis based on millions of words of tagged corpus data considers collocates of words that reliably indicate positive and negative feedback. The ordering of the analysis differs from Section 2 because we do not want to imply that there is a right or wrong way to structure this kind of multi-faceted approach. We begin though by providing an overview of patient age across the corpus.

The age of the patients who completed the National Cancer Patient Experience Survey was derived from patient records. Members of NHS England who processed the surveys converted this information into eight age-band categories prior to giving us the data in spreadsheet form (sixteen to twenty-four, twenty-five to thirty-four, thirty-five to forty-four, forty-five to fifty-four, fifty-five to sixty-four, seventy-five to eighty-four and eighty-five plus), so it is these categories on which the following analysis is based. The second and third columns of Table 8 indicate the number of patients along with the amount of words of feedback given

Table 8 Age group data for those who responded to the survey.

Age	Number of patients (%)	Total words (%)	Average rating	Female (%)	Male (%)
16–24	693 (0.32%)	54,862 (0.38%)	8.7	55.55	44.44
25–34	2,312 (1.07%)	221,140 (1.54%)	8.49	72.14	27.86
35–44	6,986 (3.25%)	654,741 (4.56%)	8.47	77.88	22.12
45–54	23,381 (10.90%)	2,071,704 (14.43%)	8.59	75.52	24.48
55–64	46,415 (21.65%)	3,574,506 (24.89%)	8.71	59.16	40.84
65–74	77,330 (36.07%)	4,914,236 (34.22%)	8.87	48.92	51.08
75–84	47,927 (22.36%)	2,427,363 (16.90%)	8.89	45.40	54.60
85+	9,296 (4.33%)	438,243 (3.05%)	8.81	46.90	53.10
Total	214,340 (100%)	14,356,795 (100%)	8.70	54.40	45.60

for each age group. It shows that for those who responded to the survey, only 6 per cent were aged forty-four and under whereas just over a third were aged forty-five to sixty-four while over half were people aged over sixty-five.

A comparative analysis that took all eight age groups into account is beyond the scope of this section, so to be consistent with the previous section, which considered two social groups (male and female patients), we decided to focus on just two age groups. Initially, we decided to compare the thirty-five to forty-four group with the seventy-five to eighty-four group as the former gave the lowest average feedback rating (8.47 on a scale of 0 to 10 where 10 is highest) and the latter gave the highest rating (8.89) as shown in the fourth column of Table 8. However, a keyword comparison of these two groups revealed many keywords that were also present when we compared comments written by male and female patients against each other (see Section 2). The last two columns in Table 8 indicate the gender distribution of patients from each age group. The thirty-five to forty-four group has the highest proportion of female patients (77.88 per cent) while the seventy-five to eighty-four group has the highest proportion of male patients (54.60 per cent). Therefore, if we compared these two age groups, the results would be partially explained by sex differences, resulting in similarities to Section 2. As such, we decided to focus on two age groups where the sex distribution was similar. The eighty-five plus age group has a reasonably comparable sex distribution to the seventy-five to eighty-four group, although this group is relatively small, contributing only 3.05 per cent of the corpus data. Additionally, a pilot analysis of this group indicated that a high proportion of the feedback was written by younger relatives of the patient, so the language use would not fully reflect people in the eighty-five plus age group. For that reason we decided to use the sixty-five to seventy-four group, which has the next closest sex split, compared to the seventy-five to eighty-four group. These groups (sixty-five to seventy-four and seventy-five to eighty-four) are the two largest in the corpus. Together they comprise 51.12 per cent of the total corpus data and 58.43 per cent of patients so our age analysis can be said to take into account the majority of patients who gave feedback.

In contrast to Section 2, where we compared men and women, using data from two adjacent age groups is perhaps less likely to result in major differences. A rationale for choosing these two age groups is that this provides a different context for comparing the findings from the sample-based and corpus-based analyses. Additionally, we want to highlight that research need not always be focussed on identifying differences.

While the two sets of analyses in Section 2 both used the keywords approach, differing on how much data was actually used, for the analysis in this section we decided to take a different approach rather than replicating the method previously used. In order to compare the age groups, for the traditional corpus analysis we took all of the comments from two age groups and focussed on collocates of the most frequent evaluative words, which would give an impression of the different aspects of their treatment that patients liked or disliked. As an equivalent approach on smaller samples where patients provided information about their age, we carried out a close reading of the data, noting by hand what they praised or criticised. We begin with the analysis of the samples.

3.2 Sample Analysis

To carry out the sample analysis of these two age groups we began by identifying 100 pieces of positive and 100 pieces of negative feedback given by people from the two age groups. For the sample analysis reported in this section, we only considered cases where patients referred to their age in their feedback. To identify such feedback, we experimented with a number of search terms, taking advantage of the fact that the corpus was part-of-speech tagged to carry out searches on phrases like *_VB* ≫3≫ 66. This produced cases where the number '66' occurred one to three words after forms of the verb 'to be' (e.g., 'I am a 66 year old man'). Most searches produced low numbers of concordance lines, so we changed the search to simply look for relevant numbers e.g. (65|66| 67|68|69|70|71|72|73|74), manually discarding irrelevant cases (which amounted to about 50 per cent of concordance lines). This technique still produced 366 lines for the sixty-five to seventy-four group and 334 lines for the seventy-five to eighty-four age group that could be used.

We expanded each concordance line that contained a relevant reference to a patient's age and then read the whole comment, noting the first positive and first negative piece of feedback within each one. While patients sometimes gave several pieces of positive and negative feedback, we wanted our samples to cover 100 separate patients and in choosing the first good or bad point that a patient mentioned we reasoned that these would be likely to be considered important issues. As we collected comments, we grouped similar ones together, gradually creating categorisation schemes for the positive and nega-tive feedback. To avoid a proliferation of categories, in cases where a category only had one occurrence, we have called this 'Other'. Table 9 shows the categories and frequencies for positive feedback.

For both age groups, the majority of positive comments related to staff with thirty-one patients in each age group praising staff in a general way, for example referring to them as *excellent* or *first class*. Staff interpersonal skills, such as being *kind* and *caring* were the second highest reason for praise among both age groups. Speed of diagnosis was also seen as important for both groups, although more patients in the sixty-five to seventy-four group mentioned this (twenty-one versus sixteen). Both groups mentioned staff technical competence and the availability of information around the same amount of time. Table 10 shows the equivalent results for negative feedback.

Patients in both age groups had a much wider range of complaints about the NHS, although here the age groups differed somewhat in the types of com-plaints mentioned. Five types of complaints were mentioned ten or more times by patients aged sixty-five to seventy-four (staff interpersonal skills, poor treatment, lack of regular check-ups, waiting times at appointments and com-munication/information). For patients aged seventy-five to eighty-four, poor aftercare, staff interpersonal skills and communication/information were men-tioned more than ten times. The largest discrepancy in negative feedback between the two age groups was the communication/information category, which was mentioned ten times by the sixty-five to seventy-four group and twenty-one times by the seventy-five to eighty-four group. Other types of feedback that involved notable discrepancies were poor aftercare (two patients versus eleven patients) and lack of regular checks for the age group (sixteen patients versus four patients).

Table 9 Positive feedback categories for age (based on qualitative analysis of samples).

Comment type	65–74	75–84	Example
Excellence of staff generally	31	31	Oncology staff work well together, are well managed and supported by a matron who is engaged in supporting staff and patients. They enjoy working as a team in a dedicated department.
Staff interpersonal skills/kindness	22	25	All the staff at [name of hospital], are caring and helpful.
Speed of diagnosis/ referral/treatment	21	16	Cancer found early! At age 66, I attended the 3year breast screening- a brilliant service.
Staff technical competence/made me well/saved my life	15	16	I owe my life to my GP who spotted I may have cancer
Information/ Communication	6	7	The A5 folder produced by professionals and patients of [name of hospital] was excellent and full of information.
Not made to feel too old for treatment	3	5	I was never made to feel that because I was over 70 when first diagnosed I would not have all appropriate treatment.
Other	2	0	Seeing different doctors.

So while staff and efficiency of treatment tended to attract positive feedback for both age groups, there was more divergence for the negative feedback, both within each group and between the two groups.

People aged sixty-five to seventy-four mentioned their age in relation to positive or negative feedback for various reasons. As noted, some patients complained about lack of regular checks for people of their age. Others noted that they have never been to hospital before despite their age – a piece of information that may be a positive self-representation technique in some cases as it positions the patient as having lived a healthy lifestyle.

Table 10 Negative feedback categories for age (based on qualitative analysis of samples).

Comment type	65–74	75–84	Example
Lack of regular checks/exclusion for my age group	16	4	Routine PSA screening of men over 65 may have diagnosed the prostate cancer earlier. / As a 72 year old woman, I had to request a mammogram myself because of age limitations.
Poor treatment	15	9	I had numerous emergency admissions post cancer treatment for side effect, due to catheter problems but all it needed was in fact the treatment I finally got. Although this operation still had to be done twice to be effective.
Staff interpersonal skills/attentiveness	12	11	Staff were not observing my recovery as outside the ward area and my curtain closed. Got up and left to sit down when I fainted alone on the floor.
Waiting times at appointments	11	8	The waiting times. Chemotherapy and radiotherapy take a long time to administer. They are tiring and debilitating in themselves. To have to wait long times before their administration is exhausting.
Communication/ Information	10	21	Continuity of staff (medical) giving information – better communication between them.
Waits for diagnosis/ appointments/ treatment	6	3	I had to pay to see a surgeon as I could not get a fast GP appointment, the surgeon saw me without a GP letter, which I was very pleased about. I was bleeding and told the receptionist but she was not able to get me an appointment quickly.

Table 10 (cont.)

Comment type	65–74	75–84	Example
Car parking/transport issues	6	5	I do feel for those families who have to drive miles to keep appointments and then have a job to find a parking space before possibly waiting longer than expected in the hospital, to be met with a horrendous bill to get their car out of the parking area.
Administrative / booking issues	4	1	The administration side was very poor. Letter to my GP had my GP's name and my own name transposed. My age was stated as 48, when I am 68 and born in 1948, spelling and grammar very poor.
Concerns not addressed	3	0	I feel my concerns about pain control weren't addressed.
Short-staffing/lack of availability	3	2	Not enough nurses for amount of patients on ward.
Sent to faraway hospital or too many hospitals	2	5	Too much travelling. I had my both operations at [name of hospital]. Then [name of hospital] for radiotherapy. Then [name of hospital] for scans. Sometimes I didn't get home till 7 o'clock at night.
Poor food	2	2	The food however, is in my opinion, inedible.
Problems with aftercare	2	11	The aftercare at home was nil. I was told a district nurse would come to my home each day to empty the drain. No one came.
Being sent surveys	0	3	No more forms, I'm 75.
Couldn't get help from GP	0	3	My own GP was no help at all. I couldn't get an appointment although I was passing blood in urine.

Table 10 (cont.)

Comment type	65–74	75–84	Example
Prescription problems	0	2	Sometimes (two occasions) pharmacy had trouble in providing any prescriptions. Waited an hour and a half on one occasion and it still had not been processed.
Other	8	10	This was my first time in hospital but I found ward life difficult due to constant noise and interruptions especially at night.

This was my first experience of a hospital and surgery (I'm 72 years!).

Other patients mentioned their age to complain about being patronised, spoken to inappropriately or ignored by staff.

Being 74 years old, found some staff, mainly nurses, spoke to my daughter instead of me.
Some other nurses were patronising, impatient and at the age of 67, I hate being addressed as 'lad' (instead of a name) by an indifferent nurse barely out of her teens.

In other cases, age was mentioned in feedback to explain why a patient needed a certain type of care (that may not have been forthcoming).

I was really glad to get out of there, but then I am 71 and very unsteady after the operation and they couldn't find a wheelchair!

Others mentioned their age as part of positive feedback, noting that they had received treatment despite their age, a point that perhaps suggests that some people over 65 may worry that they will not be prioritised or given treatment if they have cancer.

Once it was known I had cancer, I had my cancer operation in 6 weeks. I had thought that at my age (74) it might have been thought 'oh, he's too old'. Don't you believe it!

For the seventy-five to eighty-four group, patients tended to mention their age to refer to having difficulty in filling in surveys or experiencing confusion, sometimes indicating that they would have liked more support or information to have been made clearer.

> I am 82 years old and didn't get any support or extra advice.

They also mentioned lack of aftercare and difficulties in terms of transport in order to get to appointments.

> No provisions were made, I assumed there would be check-ups on me as I am 75 years old and live alone, but no such arrangements were made.

> I am 77 years old, too big a journey every day.

Additionally, these patients mentioned long waiting times, especially when they were required to arrive early in the morning and then not eat or drink before an operation that was to take place in the afternoon.

> The day of my surgery (TURP), I was asked to attend at 07:00, having fasted for excess of 6 hours. I was not called to the operating theatre until 17:00, with only sips of water throughout this period, far too long for an 80 year old.

To summarise then, the comparison of two age-related samples found quite a lot of agreement between the two groups in terms of the positive aspects of their experience, although there were more differences between the groups when they provided criticisms. Patients who mentioned their age often made it relevant to their feedback, for example by noting that their age impacted on how they were treated or how they should have been treated due to their age. We must bear in mind that we are dealing with a small amount of data though, so it is difficult to know if such results can be generalised to all patients from the two age groups.

We now turn to the corpus analysis, which made use of all of the comments in the corpus that had been tagged for the two age groups under consideration.

3.3 Corpus Analysis

In order to identify types of positive and negative feedback using corpus methods, we used collocation in order to find words that frequently occurred with evaluative words.

First, frequency lists were used to obtain the most frequent twenty positive words and the top thirty negative words in the corpus as a whole. These words were obtained by examining a frequency list of the corpus. We checked with concordances that these forty words were not used in unexpected ways. This resulted in the removal of the word *nice* from the list of positive words. Although it was a top twenty word at position sixteen, the concordance analysis revealed a high number of false positives in contexts such as 'it would be nice if' and 'not nice'. Instead, we included the word at position twenty-one: *superb*. Another word, *class*, does not immediately appear to be a positive word, although it was almost always used within the term *first class* (see Section 2),

Table 11 Frequency and distribution of positive evaluation words across the two age groups.

	65–74	**75–84**
Total uses	88,891 (18,291 per million words)	48,573 (19,626 per million words)
Total patients	51,174 out of 77,330 (66.17%)	29,854 out of 47,927 (62.28%)

so we counted this as a single word. Thus, the top twenty positive words (excluding *nice*) were *good, excellent, helpful, kind, professional, great, friendly, wonderful, brilliant, fantastic, amazing, efficient, understanding, first class, supportive, outstanding, exceptional, lovely, pleasant* and *superb*.

These words were used with proportionally similar frequencies for the two age groups and were also reasonably well distributed across the two sets of patients. The seventy-five to eighty-four group used them slightly more often while the sixty-five to seventy-four group had slightly more patients who used them (see Table 11).

We then identified the words that collocated most frequently with these positive words, collectively. We did not use a measure that indicated strength of association like Mutual Information or one based on amount of confidence that an association existed between two words, like log-likelihood, because instead we wanted to simply identify the cases of collocation that were most frequent. A span of three words either side of the search term was found to be most effective at identifying such words, allowing for cases where the subject of the evaluation occurred either after or before the evaluative word, for example 'the nurses were fantastic' versus 'Great nurses'. From the list of frequent collocates, we focussed only on nouns, removing some words that were not usually directly modified by the evaluative terms. For example, the word *hospital* appeared as a collocate but it tended to occur in statements like 'The hospital food was excellent' or 'My hospital care was first class'. In these examples, it is really the food and the care that is being evaluated. Table 12 shows the top thirty words that collocated with the positive evaluation terms for each age group.

There is not a great deal of difference between the two lists of collocates, with twenty-seven words appearing in both sets (those that only appeared in one of the lists are shown in bold). Additionally, the order of the lists is similar with most words either appearing in the same position in both lists or only one to three places away from the same position. The lists reveal that for

Table 12 Noun collocates of positive evaluation words.

Rank	65–74 Collocate	Frequency (% of comments)	75–84 Collocate	Frequency (% of comments)
1	*care*	10,327 (11.93%)	*care*	5,967 (11.36%)
2	*staff*	10,042 (11.28%)	*staff*	5,097 (9.40%)
3	*treatment*	5,241 (6.25%)	*treatment*	3,400 (6.62%)
4	*nurses*	4,706 (5.56%)	*nurses*	2,563 (4.94%)
5	*doctors*	1,796 (2.21%)	*doctors*	1,006 (2.00%)
6	*team*	1,654 (1.97%)	*service*	742 (1.44%)
7	*service*	1,312 (1.54%)	*team*	724 (1.41%)
8	*consultant*	1,214 (1.44%)	*nursing*	555 (1.06%)
9	*chemotherapy*	1,180 (1.44%)	*consultant*	536 (1.05%)
10	*nurse*	1,067 (1.30%)	*chemotherapy*	506 (1.06%)
11	*nursing*	995 (1.19%)	*job*	504 (0.99%)
12	*surgeon*	933 (1.11%)	*nurse*	480 (0.95%)
13	*people*	870 (0.99%)	*surgeon*	455 (0.86%)
14	*job*	861 (1.07%)	*people*	370 (0.70%)
15	*support*	859 (1.03%)	***attention***	352 (0.70%)
16	*GP*	745 (0.91%)	*support*	349 (0.69%)
17	*radiotherapy*	740 (0.89%)	*radiotherapy*	336 (0.65%)
18	*specialist*	619 (0.75%)	*GP*	323 (0.64%)
19	*oncology*	568 (0.68%)	*food*	317 (0.59%)
20	*consultants*	530 (0.64%)	***help***	297 (0.57%)
21	*operation*	520 (0.65%)	*specialist*	287 (0.57%)
22	*food*	500 (0.59%)	*consultants*	283 (0.56%)
23	*oncologist*	484 (0.57%)	*doctor*	259 (0.51%)
24	*manner*	476 (0.53%)	*operation*	259 (0.52%)
25	*doctor*	469 (0.57%)	*oncology*	230 (0.44%)
26	***communication***	447 (0.53%)	*Dr*	219 (0.43%)
27	***surgery***	408 (0.50%)	*manner*	209 (0.37%)
28	*Dr*	398 (0.48%)	*oncologist*	198 (0.38%)
29	*information*	392 (0.48%)	***appointments***	196 (0.39%)
30	***diagnosis***	378 (0.47%)	*information*	192 (0.39%)

both age groups, when different members of staff are evaluated positively, the word *staff* is most likely to be used, followed by *nurses* and *doctors*. However, the term *staff* is positively evaluated by 11.28 per cent of patients aged sixty-five to seventy-four and 9.40 per cent of patients aged seventy-five to eighty-four, while the younger age group was also more likely to positively evaluate *support* (1.03 per cent versus 0.69 per cent) and *GP* (0.91 per cent versus 0.64 per cent). On the other hand, the older group were more likely to positively evaluate the words *attention* (0.70 per cent versus 0.43 per cent) and *help* (0.57 per cent versus 0.34 per cent).

Concordance analyses (based on 100 random instances for each case) were used to further identify how evaluation occurred and as a result of this the collocates in Table 12 were grouped into five sets: Staff, Care, Treatment, Communication and Food. The cumulative frequencies and relative percentages of each set were calculated and are shown in Table 13. Some words only appeared in the top thirty list of one age category, for example *communication* was at twenty-sixth position for the sixty-five to seventy-four group but thirty-second position for the seventy-five to eighty-four group. For completeness, in cases like this, we considered the frequencies of *communication* for both age groups.

As with the analysis of samples shown in Table 9 earlier, Table 13 also tells a tale of similarity between the age groups as opposed to difference, with positive evaluation most likely to relate to staff in around half of cases, followed by evaluation relating to care and treatment in around a quarter of cases each. Positive evaluation relates to food and communication only around 1 per cent of the time.

A potential issue with the categorisation scheme is that the categories themselves are somewhat vague. Treatment, for example, can refer to diagnosis,

Table 13 Overall frequencies of positive evaluation categories for the two age groups.

Category	Collocates	65–74	75–84
Staff	*staff, nurses, doctors, team, consultant, nurse, surgeon, nursing, GP, people, specialist, consultants, oncologist, doctor, Dr*	26,522 (51.22%)	13,355 (48.12%)
Care	*care, support, attention, help, manner*	12,376 (23.90%)	7,174 (25.85%)
Treatment	*treatment, service, chemotherapy, job, radiotherapy, oncology, operation, surgery, diagnosis, appointments*	11,540 (22.28%)	6,525 (23.51%)
Communication	*communication, information*	839 (1.62%)	379 (1.36%)
Food	*food*	500 (0.96%)	317 (1.14%)

operations or chemotherapy, among other things. Additionally, when terms in the treatment and care categories are mentioned, they can actually sometimes relate to staff, as the following examples indicate:

> As an inpatient for a chemotherapy related side effect, I got **excellent care** from **oncology ward staff**.

> My **GP** in particular did a **great service**.

> I have always been treated in a **friendly manner** by **staff** and feel that they genuinely care.

Additionally, the staff category relates to fifteen different words relating to staff but does not reveal much about why staff were positively evaluated. It is unsurprising that staff feature so centrally in positive evaluation. Of the twenty positive evaluation words we considered, almost half of them relate particularly to qualities of staff. Seven relate to interpersonal skills or kindness: *helpful, kind, friendly, understanding, supportive, lovely* and *pleasant,* while two relate to technical competence: *professional* and *efficient.* The other eleven are more generally positive adjectives: *good, excellent, great, wonderful, brilliant, fantastic, amazing, first class, outstanding, exceptional* and *superb.* So in order to produce a more fine-grained analysis, we decided to take advantage of these three categories of positive evaluation in order to quantify which ones occur proportionally most often with different types of staff. This is shown in Table 14.

While most of the medical practitioners mentioned by patients tend to be evaluated as *excellent,* both age groups are more likely to call *doctor(s) good* (a less effusive term), while *staff* are more likely to be *friendly* and *people* are *wonderful. Staff* and *teams* are more likely to attract a wider range of positive evaluation words than the other types of practitioners. As these terms cover a larger number of people, they indicate that when most patients are positive about the different types of staff they encountered, their evaluation often covers everyone who was involved in treating them, particularly as *staff* itself attracted the most positive evaluation words for both age groups.

The preference for certain evaluative terms might be for a range of reasons. It could indicate patient perceptions that some types of staff are doing a better job or display certain positive qualities more than others, for example, both age groups use *excellent* most often to refer to *nursing* and *brilliant* to refer to their *surgeon.* However, this could also be due to the role limitations and patient expectations around different types of staff. For example, a *consultant* might be expected to listen to a patient and thus the quality of being *understanding* might be seen as more relevant to patients in this context, explaining why patients aged seventy-five to eighty-four were

Table 14 Positive evaluation relating to staff via age group.

	Positive term most likely to be used 65–74/ 75–84	Most likely than other medical practitioners to be called 64–74	Most likely than other medical practitioners to be called 75–84
staff	*friendly/ excellent*	*helpful, kind, friendly, understanding, pleasant, efficient*	*helpful, kind, friendly, pleasant, supportive, efficient*
people	*wonderful/ wonderful*	*lovely, wonderful*	*lovely, wonderful*
team	*excellent/ excellent*	*supportive, professional, great, fantastic, amazing, outstanding, exceptional*	*professional, great, fantastic, amazing, first class, exceptional*
surgeon	*excellent/ excellent*	*brilliant, first class*	*brilliant*
oncologist	*excellent/good*	*superb*	*outstanding*
nurses	*excellent/good*	*good*	—
nursing	*excellent/ excellent*	*excellent*	*good, excellent, superb*
nurse	*excellent/ excellent*	—	—
consultant	*excellent/ excellent*	—	*understanding*
consultants	*excellent/ excellent*	—	—
GP	*excellent/ excellent*	—	—
Dr	*excellent/ excellent*	—	—
doctor	*good/good*	—	—
doctors	*good/good*	—	—
specialist	*good/excellent*	—	—

most likely to evaluate their consultant in this way, compared to other staff members. It might also be the case that patients are unconsciously drawing on linguistic forms of evaluation that circulate in society. The fact that *doctor(s)* are called *good* more than *excellent* (which goes against the usual pattern for most staff members) may be due to people's previous encounters with language. In the British National Corpus (introduced in Section 1), *doctor* collocates with *good* 106 times while it only collocates with *excellent* twice. Also in the BNC, *surgeon* collocates with *brilliant* twice, although it never collocates with any of the other nineteen evaluative words we considered in this part of the analysis.

Considering the three groups of positive evaluation words, we can consider how they are distributed across the staff words collectively, for the two age groups, as shown in Table 15.

Table 15 indicates that when patients praise staff both age groups favour the general positive words like *excellent* (a finding that was expected considering that these words comprised eleven out of the top twenty most frequent evaluative words). Interpersonal words are used about a quarter of the time and (perhaps surprisingly, considering their importance) technical competence words are least likely to be used. The table also indicates that there is little difference between the two age groups in these relative frequencies.

This is a slightly different picture from the qualitative analysis, which indicated a slight preference for the seventy-five to eighty-four group to praise staff for their interpersonal qualities but did not find any age-group differences in terms of use of general positive evaluation. However, the qualitative analysis did identify staff as being the most common subject of positive evaluations in both groups. The corpus analysis, being based on a much larger data-set, and taking into account fifteen types of staff across twenty terms of evaluation, is likely to give a more accurate picture than the one based on comparing two sets of 100 pieces of feedback. Bearing this in mind, we now move on to consider negative feedback.

To identify complaints, we first identified the twenty most frequent negative evaluative words across the whole corpus: *poor, bad, awful, terrible, rude, appalling, unacceptable, aggressive, noisy, dreadful, inadequate, insensitive,*

Table 15 Evaluation categories (percentages) for staff words collectively by age group.

	65–74	75–84
Interpersonal words	27.9%	26.2%
Technical competence	6.7%	4.9%
General positive	65.3%	68.8%

Table 16 Frequency and distribution of negative evaluation words across the two age groups.

	65–74	75–84
Total uses	6,992 (1,422 per million words)	2,906 (1,174 per million words)
Total patients	5,799 out of 77,330 (7.49%)	2,479 out of 47,927 (5.17%)

abrupt, disappointing, horrible, horrendous, unhelpful, disgusting, insufficient and *chaotic*. Table 16 shows the collective frequencies and distributions for these words across the two age groups.

Compared to frequencies of the positive evaluative words (Table 11), the negative ones are much less common. This reveals a finding that was not made by the earlier qualitative analysis – the extent to which both age groups give positive versus negative feedback. The difference between the amount of positive versus negative evaluation is slightly wider for the seventy-five to eighty-four group, compared to the sixty-five to seventy-four group.

We identified the words (again, only focussing on nouns) that collocated most frequently with these negative words. As with the positive evaluation words, a span of three words either side of the search term was found to be most effective, allowing for cases like 'food really bad' and 'bad at communication'. We removed some collocates from the list we obtained as they were not actually the subject of evaluation, for example the word *cancer* occurred as a collocate but tended to refer to cases like 'food on the cancer wards was disgusting'.

A potential problem with this method is that these strongly negative evaluative words tended to be used most frequently by a small number of patients (7.49 per cent of the sixty-five to seventy-four age group and 5.17 per cent of the seventy-five to eighty-four group). Overall, these negative words are four times more likely to be used by patients who gave a satisfaction rating of zero as opposed to a rating of ten. Patients who gave low ratings tended to be very direct in their evaluations, as demonstrated by the following example, from a patient who gave a rating of zero.

The attitude of the consultant was bad. The anaesthetist was rude and arrogant.

On the other hand, patients who gave higher ratings tended to be more indirect in their criticisms, as illustrated by the following patient who gave a rating of ten.

> Communication could have been improved for, especially as my ability to
> wake is still currently affected and I need to consider future work/change of
> type work in relation to this.

This criticism contains no overtly evaluative word, although it is clear that
communication is being negatively evaluated. Instead, the modal verb *could* is
used to hedge the criticism, along with a positive word, *improved*. Additionally,
a reason is given for the criticism. This politer form of negative evaluation would
be missed if we only considered the more obviously negative cases. This would
not be problematic if there were only a few cases like this. However, overall,
almost 40 per cent of patients gave a score of ten, 30 per cent gave a score of nine,
and 20 per cent gave a score of eight. These patients tended to avoid the overtly
negatively evaluative words, instead using more hedged forms of criticism. To
take the views of these patients into account, we considered other words that
indicated criticisms by scanning concordance lines of the top 100 most frequent
words in the corpus in order to identify words that might be useful in revealing
patterns of evaluation. Three words that proved to be productive were *could*,
would and *more*. Concordance analyses indicated that these three words were
often (but not always) used in criticisms, involving suggestions for improvement.

We therefore decided to identify the most frequent collocates of these three
words in order to ascertain the kinds of complaints that the two age groups
made. As with the previous search on the top twenty negative words, not all
collocates were of use, so we filtered out grammatical collocates. Additionally,
some collocates resulted in false positives, as the following examples attest
(collocational pairs are shown in bold).

> My oncologist and staff generally could not have been **more** caring and
> **helpful**.
>
> **Could** not **fault** the surgeon.
>
> I **could** recommend **treatment** and service received was very sensitive and
> caring.
>
> It was explained to me that **treatment would** be palliative.

While the right-hand collocates of *more* were reasonably productive in terms
of eliciting criticisms (apart from obviously positive words like *helpful*), there
were too many false positives for cases of *could* and *would*. Therefore, we
considered frequent clusters of these words. Across the whole corpus, the most
frequent three-word cluster of *could* was *could have been*, and this search
contained far fewer false positives when its collocates were examined, particularly when considering just the left-hand collocates. The fifth most frequent
cluster – *could be improved* – was similarly useful to examine. For *would*, no

three-word clusters were found to produce many criticisms, although the two-word cluster *would have* (when searched on a span of five words to the left) was found to be most productive, as well as returning a low number of false positives in its collocates list. We therefore identified the most frequent collocates for these four search terms (removing false positives), for the two age groups under consideration. The top ten collocates for each search term (including the original search on the top twenty negative evaluative words) are shown in Table 17.

For both groups, the word *staff* occurred most frequently, appearing collect-ively 1,421 times for the sixty-five to seventy-four group and 553 times for the seventy-five to eighty-four group. The majority of these cases occurred with the word *more*, indicating cases where patients complained about under-staffing as opposed to cases where staff were actually criticised via evaluative words like *terrible* or phrases like 'staff could be improved'.

> Overall care is excellent, but there are times it seems there should be **more staff** in the clinic.

Of the three types of complaint, when the sixty-five to seventy-four age group mention staff, 17.66 per cent of the time they use an explicitly negative evaluation term, 77.48 per cent of the time they complain about under-staffing and 4.87 per cent of the time they give a polite criticism. These figures are 16.09 per cent, 81.19 per cent and 2.71 per cent for the seventy-five to eighty-four group, indicating that there is not a huge amount of difference between the two groups.

After *staff*, both groups complained most about *nurses*, *time*, *care* and *food*. However, we decided that a more inclusive approach would be to group related words into categories. For example, a category called 'Staff' could include the words *staff*, *nurses*, *nursing*, *doctors*, *doctors* and *GP*. Along with Staff, we identified six other categories from Table 17: Information, Care, Waiting times, Treatment, Facilities and System. The constituent words and collective frequen-cies of these seven categories for the two age groups are shown in Table 18.

The last two columns of Table 18 indicate that proportionally there is little difference in the age groups in terms of the complaints they make. Most common for both groups are complaints about staff, followed by information, care, waiting times, treatment, facilities then system. The largest difference is for facilities, which comprises 8.04 per cent of complaints for the seventy-five to eighty-four group and 5.45 per cent for the sixty-five to seventy-four group, although even here, the difference is not huge.

It is notable that the categories of complaint and praise found with the corpus analysis are much more general than those found with the qualitative

Table 17 Collocates indicating criticisms.

Search term (span)	65–74 age group collocates (frequency)	75–84 age group collocates (frequency)
Collocates of top 20 negative words (R3–L3)	*food* (251), *staff* (251), *care* (210), *communication* (177), *time* (137), *nurses* (135), *administration* (126), *GP* (123), *times* (122), *parking* (104)	*food* (120), *care* (91), *staff* (89), *parking* (77), *communication* (68), *nurses* (66), *times* (58), *GP* (56), *time* (55), *administration* (53)
more (R1–R3)	*staff* (1,102), *information* (714), *nurses* (637), *time* (292), *help* (226), *care* (198), *support* (193), *money* (142), *nursing* (141), *doctors* (132)	*staff* (449), *information* (342), *nurses* (316), *time* (138), *help* (110), *care* (100), *doctors* (79), *nursing* (70), *money* (69), *support* (63)
could have been (L3–L1)	*treatment* (99), *care* (70), *operation* (65), *GP* (62), *diagnosis* (61), *time* (40), *staff* (31), *appointments* (29), *food* (26), *communication* (26)	*treatment* (50), *care* (33), *GP* (33), *diagnosis* (23), *ward* (21), *information* (18), *operation* (15), *communication* (14), *food* (14), *times* (14)
could be improved (L3–L1)	*times* (39), *administration* (35), *waiting* (33), *communication* (31), *appointment* (25), *care* (23), *treatment* (20), *appointments* (20), *food* (20), *system* (17)	*waiting* (32), *times* (30), *time* (16), *communication* (15), *food* (15), *care* (10), *administration* (10), *treatment* (10), *appointments* (8), *pharmacy* (7)
would have (R1–R5)	*information* (107), *treatment* (84), *time* (65), *care* (41), *GP* (39), *staff* (37), *appointment* (37), *help* (37), *radiotherapy* (33), *nurse* (33)	*information* (54), *treatment* (38), *help* (23), *time* (22), *staff* (15), *scan* (14), *doctor* (12), *nurse* (12), *appointment* (11), *GP* (10)

analysis. The qualitative analysis found that the sixty-five to seventy-four group complained about a lack of regular screenings for people in their age group. None of the collocates in Table 18 were suggestive of this kind of complaint though. Indeed, when we examined instances where patients

Table 18 Overall frequencies of negative evaluation categories
for the two age groups.

Category	Words in category	65–74 frequency	75–84 frequency
Staff	*staff, nurse, nurses, nursing, doctors, doctors, GP*	2,588 (39.63%)	1,207 (39.29%)
Information	*information, communication*	1,055 (16.15%)	511 (16.63%)
Care	*care, help, support*	998 (15.28%)	430 (13.99%)
Waiting times	*waiting, time, times, appointment, appointments*	839 (12.85%)	384 (12.50%)
Treatment	*treatment, scan, results, diagnosis, radiotherapy, operation*	365 (5.58%)	150 (4.88%)
Facilities	*food, parking, ward*	356 (5.45%)	247 (8.04%)
System	*system, administration, pharmacy*	329 (5.03%)	143 (4.65%)

made this complaint, we did not find evaluative adjectives being used, as the following examples indicate.

> My comment is that maybe males should be checked for PSA after a certain age so as to be able to operate or whatever. I am 73.

> All males should have a test for prostate cancer after the age of 30 years or advised to have a test for cancer.

> Young women should have breast screening from early age.

These examples all contain the word *should*, although this was not one of the words we searched for, as it would have resulted in too many false positives appearing. However, even if we had included *should*, it would have resulted in collocates like *scan*, *test* and *screening* appearing, which we would have categorised as 'Treatment' in Table 18. Reading concordance lines of the collocational pairs of *should + scan*, *test* or *screening* would at least have revealed the more specific types of complaint, allowing for the potential of a more fine-grained categorisation system but this would have meant that many hundreds of concordance lines would have to be read, with the analysis becoming more akin to the qualitative one, just on a much larger scale.

3.4 Conclusion

The overall picture from the comparison of two age groups was more of similarity than difference, with the corpus approach in particular showing up hardly any differences. This is perhaps to be expected: the two age groups chosen for analysis are adjacent to one another and patients from both groups are thus likely to access similar types of services and are perhaps also likely to have similar concerns. Analysts can sometimes be geared towards identifying differences and corpus tools like keywords can prioritise difference-motivated research. However, similarities should not be dismissed as non-findings out of hand, especially if it is assumed that certain differences will be found.

The comparison of the qualitative and corpus approaches to the age group analysis indicated both similarities and differences between the two approaches. For positive evaluations, the qualitative analysis identified a small number of categories with staff being the main subject of praise in both age groups, followed by speed that a patient was treated, referred or diagnosed (slightly more common in the sixty-five to seventy-four age group) and technical competence. The corpus analysis also found that both groups were most likely to give praise related to staff, with care and treatment each being about half as common. Praise related to communication and information was much less frequent, comprising only about 1 per cent of the positive evaluation found, as was the case for food. The corpus analysis also indicated some of the ways that different types of staff were evaluated positively, for example with doctors likely to be described as *good* when people gave them praise, while surgeons were more likely than any other staff member to be labelled *brilliant*.

For the negative evaluations, the corpus approach found few differences between age groups, with staff comprising around 40 per cent of complaints, followed by information, care and waiting times (each comprising around 15 per cent). Then facilities, system and treatment all comprised 3–8 per cent each. The corpus analysis identified three types of complaint that could be used to further categorise negative evaluation. Negative adjectives like *dreadful* and *chaotic* indicated cases where patients went on-record (usually in quite angry ways) about a particular aspect of their experience. However, another form of criticism involved noting a lack of something, commonly indicated via the word *more*, while phrases like *could be improved* and *could have been* were used by patients to give a more polite form of criticism, usually by people who were, overall, reasonably happy with their experience. Such phrases were developed by examining the most frequent words and their clusters in the corpus. However, a more thorough analysis could have spent longer developing other terms that indicated criticism (e.g. *not enough*, *should have been*). One issue with the corpus analysis is that it is difficult to know if we have caught every instance of a phenomenon. Another issue is that unless we carry out scrupulous analysis of every concordance line, we may end up inflating our numbers by counting unwanted cases.

The qualitative approach found a different picture around complaints. The sixty-five to seventy-four age group complained most about being excluded from treatment or scans due to their age. This was not a concern that was identified with the corpus analysis though. Other non-age-related complaints were found to be across both groups – such as complaints about staff and waiting times – a similar picture to the corpus analysis. However, the qualitative approach found large differences between age groups relating to communication/information and aftercare, with the seventy-five to eighty-four group citing these more often than the sixty-five to seventy-four group. The corpus analysis did not note the higher rate of seventy-five to eighty-four complaints about information and did not pick up at all on complaints around aftercare.

The qualitative analysis uncovered more specific reasons for complaints. For example, categories involved aspects like 'lack of aftercare' while the corpus analysis resulted in what could be seen as equivalent but broader categories like 'care'. A related difference was that the qualitative analysis resulted in more refinement of categories producing 17 categories of complaint. The actual number of original categories was even higher than this. As some categories only contained a single instance of a complaint, they were grouped together in a catch-all category called 'Other'. Additionally, to avoid proliferation of categories, other categories were grouped together (such as staff interpersonal skills and staff attentiveness). The qualitative analysis therefore risks becoming too fine-grained, with so many categories that it is difficult to determine what the main concerns actually are. However, the corpus analysis that focussed on grouping words resulted in only seven main categories, giving a broader but more reductive analysis, which may be equally problematic.

A potential issue with the qualitative analysis is that only a small number of patients referred to their age in their comments and when they did so it was sometimes to make comments that were related to their age. This resulted in feedback that is helpful in distinguishing age groups (e.g. the sixty-five to seventy-four group mentioned the lack of regular checks for their age group more than the seventy-five to eighty-four group) although such feedback is unlikely to be very frequent so is actually quite unrepresentative overall, particularly when we consider that such age-related concerns did not appear within the corpus analysis. Therefore, researchers who are tasked to analyse demographic-related data like age via self-references might want to flag cases where age is made an issue as opposed to more casual mentions of age. The former may not be as likely to be representative of the whole population.

However, a problem with trying to make quantitative generalisations from a small qualitative analysis (in this case, involving sets of 100 cases) is that some categories are likely to be over- or under-represented, compared to the whole corpus. We can at least be more confident that an analysis based on the whole dataset is likely to give a more accurate account of the proportional differences between categories found. So from the corpus analysis we are able to conclude that for both age groups complaints about staff are about twice as frequent as complaints about communication. However, this leads to another issue: how much is that really telling us? Would it be more useful to know about specific problematic aspects of evaluation? What kinds of complaints are there about staff or communication, in other words?

In the final section we compare our findings from the two approaches further, considering their pros and cons, as well as attempting to outline ways that the analysis could have been optimised.

4 Conclusion and Reflections

In this Element, we have reported analyses of the language of patient feedback on NHS cancer care services in England. In particular, we approached these texts from the perspective of identity, and specifically the identity variables of sex and age. In Section 2, we compared the feedback provided by male patients with that provided by female patients (and vice versa), while in Section 3 we compared comments provided by patients from two age groups (sixty-five to seventy-four and seventy-five to eighty-four). The analysis in those sections highlighted both similarities and differences between the groups under focus, both in terms of the themes of their comments and the language they use to present themselves and to evaluate their experiences. We have, where relevant, interpreted those patterns as reflecting particularities about the type of care typically accessed by these groups, as well as in terms of wider discourses around these social groups and how these are drawn upon by patients both in the construction of their subjectivities but also in their evaluations of care. This can lead to an intersection between these areas of discursive representation, with notions and constructions of identity enmeshing with and influencing the linguistic evaluation of healthcare services given in the feedback.

Patients' identities and the ways they constructed these in their comments could therefore have ramifications for how they evaluated healthcare services, including the types of linguistic strategies they used to frame this evaluation, to contextualise their perspectives and to legitimise their arguments. While our analysis focussed mostly on difference, we should also try not to lose sight of the similarities between the groups we examined (and others), and indeed some of these were visible in our analyses. We underscore at this point the need for healthcare providers and feedback monitors to be cognisant of the capacity for patients' discursive identity constructions to shape how they give feedback and linguistically evaluate their experiences. Some linguistic strategies may seem more convincing or representative than others, as well as being associated with a particular sex-related, age-related or other identity-based style. It is important to be mindful of this, as it may result in the perspectives of some groups being given precedence over others, or being more likely to lead to changes in practices or policies. Which strategies will be more appealing will depend on who is reading and acting on them. The relationship between identity and linguistic evaluation is, to our knowledge, an under-studied topic. More linguistic research in this area in the future could help to develop such critical literacy, particularly if that work takes an applied focus and engages with stakeholders involved in collecting and processing such texts.

As well as setting out to shed new light on the influence of identity on written healthcare feedback, through the analysis in this Element we also aimed to explore several more general issues around the study of identity in corpora. For the remainder of this section, then, we attempt to address these issues. First, we consider the efficacy of working with socio-demographic data. Second, we look at the pros and cons of the sample-based and corpus approaches. Then, finally, we consider how the different approaches could work together.

Beginning with the first of these issues then, through our analyses in Sections 2 and 3 we compared two approaches to identifying and analysing identity in a corpus: one relying on the use of socio-demographic metadata annotations and the other using patients' references to their sex- and age-related identities. At this point, then, we can ask: in terms of how to deal with corpus data that is not tagged with sociolinguistic variables, how effective was it to work with small samples where people self-declared their age or sex? In Section 2, we took two approaches to analysing the influence of patients' sex: one that relied on sex-related metadata tags and another approach in which keywords were derived from relatively small samples of data where people had self-declared their sex in their comments.

The keywords obtained from looking at the smaller sample of data produced completely different (although perhaps complementary) results to the keywords from all data tagged as male or female and in one case a contradictory result, whereby *I* was key for the male sample as well as being key for the larger female corpus. The keywords obtained through the full corpus comparison indicated differences that were telling in terms of how gender related to more general concerns and feedback strategies, with male patients being more concerned with processes and aiming to make their feedback appear generalised and female patients being more feeling-based and interested in relationships with staff. On the other hand, when the keywords of the samples (where sex or gender was made explicit) were examined, other strategies were revealed in terms of how patients used authorial voice. Here, male patients referred to themselves with *I* whereas female patients positioned themselves as acted on by others via *me*. This finding mirrors language use in heterosexual women's personal adverts (see Baker, 2017). However, *me* did not appear when all the male and female feedback was compared together, so we cannot be certain that this is a generalisable finding. Obviously, the more data we have to analyse, the more confident we can be about our claims.

An advantage of the sample-based approach was that the patients' mentions of their sex identities in their comments arguably gave us a set of texts in which gendered discourses were more clearly relevant to the comments and, in turn, to the differences we found between the male and female patients' feedback. Indeed, in orienting to their sex, patients frequently drew on explicitly gendered discourses in order to construct their identities and to interpret, explain and evaluate their experiences of healthcare. By contrast, the comparison of male and female patients based on sex-related metadata tags, while also revealing of gendered discourses to an extent, arguably proved to be more useful for exploring differences in gendered style.

The fact that some patients do explicitly reference their sex or age gives us some confidence that these variables are relevant ones and worth involving in larger-scale comparative analysis. In some cases these explicit mentions of sex or age could help with the interpretation of the analysis carried out on the tagged data. Relying on patients' mentions of (aspects of) their identities can provide something of a warrant that that identity variable is relevant to the patterns being observed, as language users have oriented to these themselves, although care should be taken not to assume that patients who explicitly mention their sex or age are typical of the wider population.

Another benefit of the sample-based approach to identifying patients' sex was that the patients' orientations to one identity category frequently accompanied, or even gave rise to, another. In particular, we found in Section 2 that patients who referenced aspects of their sex identity – either as men or women – were also particularly likely to reference their age too. This was not an expected finding, but it is one that demonstrates the possibility for the referencing of one identity category to occur alongside another. Analysts could utilise such self-references to identity categories as a basis on which to decide what aspects of identity to look at in their analysis. We will return to this possibility at the end of this section. As well as giving rise to unexpected (but relevant) areas for analytical focus, patients' co-occurring mentions of particular identity categories also brought us closer to appreciating intersectional aspects of identity and which aspects of their identities patients thought were relevant to their experiences, or which ones they drew upon in conjunction with one another in order to understand, explain and evaluate their experiences. It was clear, for example, that a fair number of the male and female patients in our samples felt that at times that both their sex and age identities, together, were relevant to given experiences of healthcare, or otherwise found it beneficial to verbally invoke both of these aspects of their identities together for rhetorical effect. Intersectionality is a particularly complex phenomenon and accounting for it in a large corpus can be challenging. We should be careful not to dismiss the possible relevance of a particular aspect of identity, or combination of aspects, simply on the basis that a language user has not oriented to this explicitly. However, the sample-based approach could provide a promising analytical entry point through which analysts can not only determine analytical categories for focus but also explore the issue of intersectionality.

Although it bore some advantages for our analysis, the sample-based approach also had some limitations. The first concerns the size of the samples that this approach enabled us to work with. Because patients' referring to or declaring certain aspects of their identities in their comments was relatively infrequent in the corpus, the sample-based approach forced us to work with very small samples of comments in both Sections 2 and 3. This poses an immediate challenge from a corpus linguistics perspective, not only as it is likely to hinder the generalisability of our findings (an issue we return to shortly) but also practical challenges in terms of the techniques we were able to use. For example, in Section 2, perhaps due to the small corpus sizes, no keywords were found when the male sample was compared against the female sample (and vice versa). This indicates one of the potential issues with trying to carry out corpus procedures by comparing together two small datasets (in our case, the two samples came to 34,000 words when added together). However, when we compared each of these sample corpora against all the patient feedback we had, keywords did emerge, revealing some interesting differences and similarities between the two samples of feedback. Still, it resulted in a small number of low-frequency keywords and it is uncertain that our findings would be replicated if we had collected other samples of people who declared their sex in their feedback.

In Section 3, there was no attempt to carry out corpus procedures on the two samples of feedback where people declared their age and instead the feedback was read line by line and praise and criticisms were categorised by hand. Again, this resulted in small frequencies, along with quite a fine-grained categorisation system, which on the one hand allowed for detail but on the other also makes it difficult to make claims of representativeness, even just for people who declare their age in their feedback, let alone for all people of those age groups. Some of these categories could perhaps have been combined together, resulting in higher frequencies, although there is always going to be a trade-off between the number of categories and their frequency, and we can be less certain of representativeness when frequencies are low.

The corpus analysis of age had the opposite problem; collocates were grouped into a smaller number of general categories that were perhaps not useful if particular concerns wanted to be addressed. Additionally, without carrying out careful checks of every concordance line, it is difficult to be certain that a pair of collocates always represented the kind of praise or complaint that they were categorised as. We can make a more confident claim to generalisability as we are dealing with hundreds of cases, although when we talk of relatively broad categories like 'staff' or 'care' we cannot be certain as to what exactly we are generalising.

Another issue with the samples is due to the way they are collected. When people go on-record about their age or sex, it is often because these qualities are central to the type of feedback they are giving. In Section 2, for example, we noted how a female patient who praised staff for treating her as an intelligent woman could be interpreted as implying that she did not expect this to be the case, indicating that her feedback oriented to a discourse of sexism. Similarly, in Section 3, we found that when patients mentioned their age, it was often to give praise or make a complaint in relation to it, for example concern that their age group was not offered routine scans. Such cases are interesting and arguably important but as they did not emerge with the corpus analyses of the full datasets they could also be seen as fairly atypical, as most patients in the corpus did *not* mention their age. It could be argued, though, that the technique used to identify evaluation in the corpus analysis (collocations with evaluative adjectives or phrases like *could have been*) was not good at revealing cases of patients complaining about not being offered routine scans, while another technique might have found them.

Still, we would urge caution in terms of making claims about generalisability when working with small samples where people self-declare an identity trait. What emerges may not be typical of the majority of cases where such traits are not made explicit. Having a corpus that is tagged for socio-demographic information, ideally in its entirety or at least for the majority of the texts/ language users it contains, may seem an obvious way of working with a more widely representative dataset. Indeed, the annotation-based analyses we carried out, by virtue of their accounting for a far larger portion of the data, meant that we could be more confident about the generalisability of the findings we arrived at through this approach. Moreover, that the tags accounted for a diverse range of identity aspects also helped us to better evaluate the socio-demographic balance of our data more reliably and more comprehensively than we would have been able to do through the self-reference-based approach alone. This was useful in Section 3, for example, for us to be aware of the socio-demographic imbalance of certain age groups with respect to the degree to which male and female patients were represented. Similarly, the intersection of age and sex, as reflected in the socio-demographic metadata available to us, gave us otherwise unobtainable explanatory power when accounting for some of the stylistic differences between male and female patients' comments we observed in Section 2, where the older make-up of the male patients in our data likely resulted in a marked use of certain forms of language associated with older age groups in these comments.

For undertaking a large-scale quantitative analysis of language and identity, then, there are clear advantages of taking an annotation-based approach. However, this approach also has some limitations. On a practical level, reliably annotating a large corpus for socio-demographic metadata is no straightforward task and the larger the corpus we are analysing, the more resource-intensive this endeavour becomes. We were helped in this regard by our collaboration with NHS England as our contacts there had collected reliable socio-demographic metadata at the point at which the feedback was given. This was then provided to us in a format whereby it was relatively straightforward to convert this metadata into a series of searchable tags for each comment.

Another criticism of socio-demographic annotations is that they frequently depend on social categories that, for the facility of analysis, are broad (e.g. men and women) but whose breadth may result in overly simplistic views of identity categories. In the National Cancer Patient Experience Survey, respondents were asked to answer questions relating to a range of identity categories: age, sex, ethnicity, sexuality, health condition and whether English was their first language. We can therefore (potentially) analyse and compare these categories because patients were asked about them. However, we did note that some of the socio-demographic variables could have different meanings for those contributing comments in our corpus. We found comments in the feedback like 'Did not appreciate questions about my sexuality or my ethnic roots. I completed this survey to help with cancer care, nothing else.' Patients were much more likely to answer questions about age and sex as opposed to sexuality or ethnicity, which were sometimes left blank or patients ticked the option 'prefer not to say'. As a result, we have much less data for some of these socio-demographic variables than others and what we do have is self-selecting. Additionally, we noted intersectional aspects when it came to answering socio-demographic questions. For example, younger patients were more likely to provide some sort of answer to the question about sexual identity (although they were also more likely than any other group to answer with 'prefer not to say'), whereas older patients, particularly those aged above fifty-five, were more likely to tick none of the options when asked about their sexuality. This means that some aspects of socio-demographic identity are going to be easier to analyse than others, due to questions about them appearing in surveys and participants being willing (or not) to disclose those aspects of identity. Ironically, it is perhaps the identity groups like sexuality and ethnicity, where there is more of a taboo or concern about disclosure, where work is needed in order to address issues around bias or discrimination.

A further limitation of this approach relates to a more general criticism made of studies based on correlation between social categories and language use. Specifically, statistically significant correlations between a social attribute and the use of a linguistic feature is often interpreted as a relationship of causation. However, as Swann (2002) argues, the marked use of a linguistic feature by members of a social group may be related not (just) to the aspect of identity under analytical focus but to some other aspect of the language users' identity. In this study, we focussed on just two aspects of social identity (sex and age), but in a fuller study of identity we could have combined different socio-demographic annotations together in order to glean a more comprehensive understanding of whether and how different aspects of identity culminate to produce particular forms of language use in this context. Yet even if we had taken such an approach, no set of socio-demographic annotations is ever complete. Indeed, there are numerous other aspects of identity that the patients in our study could have been asked about but were not and some of these factors – like social class, for example – are notoriously tricky to categorise due to their particularly fluid and subjective nature. With this kind of survey data, then, we are restricted by what the survey creators decided were important to ask.

Another limitation of the large-scale annotation-based corpus studies of identities is that what may be gained in scalability and practicality might be lost in granularity, as broad social category annotations are likely to enforce top-down conceptions of identity, which are suitably broad to be applied across a large corpus but that may, in the process, obscure from our analytical view the more nuanced types of identity relations that can arise in local contexts. Indeed, Bucholtz and Hall (2005) point out how linguistic ethnographers have 'repeatedly demonstrated that language users often orient to local identity categories rather than to the analyst's sociological categories and that the former frequently provide a better empirical account of linguistic practice'. To an extent, self-reference-based approaches, such as that we have used in this Element, can help us to buttress against an over-reliance on correlational perspectives, as the language users' local orientations to given identity categories allow, as noted, for more fluid and intersectional identity categories to be developed, in turn bringing the analyst closer to which aspects of identity language users themselves consider to be relevant, and where.

A pertinent question to ask at this point, then, pertains to which approach would be recommended for researchers who, like us, are studying the relationship between language and identity in a large corpus of texts. The answer would depend on the level of granularity and/or accuracy required, as well as the data itself. If the socio-demographic variable(s) of interest are not tagged or otherwise available across the whole dataset, then a qualitative approach based on identifying self-declared cases of age, sex and so on will at least offer numerous detailed categories, although care would need to be taken regarding generalisability, and those categories that are focussed on the demographic variable are likely to be less typical than frequencies would have us believe. If we have access to tagged socio-demographic metadata then an approach based first on identifying common forms of evaluation based on words and phrases and then examining their collocates and possibly grouping similar collocates together will give a more accurate picture, albeit one that does not provide much detail. Such an approach could also provide the basis for a more qualitative approach, for example examining concordance lines containing cases where an evaluative word collocates with words from a particular category. For cases that produced hundreds of concordance lines, a sampling approach would reduce the amount of work required, for example for each concordance search, a random sample of twenty, fifty or 100 lines could be read.

Another approach could be to try to combine the two methods we have detailed here in some way. Particularly if we were working with a corpus that is tagged for socio-demographic information, we would not necessarily have to only look at a sample containing cases where people explicitly mention their age or sex, but we could just take 100 random cases from everyone tagged from a particular socio-demographic category. Then the more detailed forms of evaluation found from the qualitative analysis could be used to inform the broader findings from the corpus analysis. For example, in Section 3, we found that both age groups complained most about staff. However, from the qualitative analysis we found that complaints about staff tended to be focussed around interpersonal skills and staff neglect. Similarly, the corpus analysis in Section 3 identified a category that we called 'Care', while the qualitative analysis of the sample indicated that aftercare was particularly a concern of one age group. Matching up categories in this way would help to provide finer granularity along with the accuracy based on the larger numbers.

Yet even if we do have access to reliable socio-demographic metadata, for example in the form of socio-demographic annotation, this does not necessarily mean that there is not also a place for the kinds of self-reference-based approach utilised in parts of the foregoing analysis (and in Baker et al., 2019). Having at our avail a wide range of socio-demographic tags can make an analyst feel like a child in a sweet shop, not knowing which aspect of identity or identity variables to consider in their analysis. In such cases, we envisage how mentions of particular identity aspects in the texts within the corpus could help in determining areas for analytical focus. Such a bottom-up approach has the advantage in giving us a data-driven warrant for exploring certain identity categories, being selected for example because they are the most frequent ones, thereby reducing the chances that analysts focus on categories that they find interesting, but that are not actually that relevant to the language users represented in their data.

One way we could do this would be to search for the frequency of certain identity labels and then focus, through analysis utilising socio-demographic tags, on the variables that are most likely to be noted as salient by the language users in our corpus themselves. Another, more bottom-up approach, would involve looking closely at a sample of texts in the corpus and noting emergent identity categories that could then form the focus on an annotation-based analysis. A benefit of this approach is that it may help us to account for more subtle or even implied forms of identity self-referencing that may otherwise be overlooked by the kinds of frequency searches described above. Such an approach may also bring us closer to observing intersectional aspects of identity, where we see whether certain identity categories tend to be implicitly or explicitly referenced in conjunction with one another. Whichever approach we opt for, one limitation seems to be that as soon as we start scaling up our corpus analysis, we naturally lose sight of some emergent identity categories, with more implicit instances of identity marking, for example around variables like social class in particular, being perhaps the most likely to be at risk of being overlooked altogether. Additionally, identity characteristics like sexuality may receive less attention, perhaps because the majority of the population view their own sexual identity as heterosexual (the unmarked case) while those with non-heterosexual identities may be less willing to disclose them. Frequency should not be the only indicator of importance then and should be supplemented with a qualitative aspect to the analysis that looks at how identity groups are oriented to (e.g. it is notable that people complained about the questions on sexuality and ethnicity).

Taken together, then, the self-reference-based approach can give our analysis focus, guard against critical overreliance on correlational statistics and narrow the gap between our observations and interpretations, while reliable metadata can give us scalability and help us to assess the demographic balance of a corpus, in turn helping us to guard against the influence of strong imbalances. Therefore, we would say that if you have metadata, you can still find use for approaches that examine smaller samples in a more qualitative way. However, large-scale annotation can be time-consuming and expensive, so it is sometimes not possible to reliably code a corpus for such information, for example because its contributors are anonymous (e.g. with some forms of social media data). In such cases, the self-reference-based approach can be useful, but we need to be mindful of its limitations, which we have discussed throughout this section.

We conclude, then, with the view that a corpus-based approach to comparing socio-demographic categories in data like patient feedback has value, although there is potential to make claims that are too general or to miss the whole picture. Complementing the annotation-based approach with searches for identity references, as well as combining a whole-corpus approach with one in which we work more closely with samples would, we argue, likely to help us to fill in some of the gaps and ultimately provide a richer account of our data. In numerous contexts, people are asked to provide feedback, from something as banal as having a plumber fix a sink to more life-changing contexts like cancer treatment. It is important then, that those who are tasked with making sense of this feedback are provided with workable techniques of analysing it, so that they can make appropriate recommendations for improvements. We hope that this Element has identified how some of these techniques may be utilised.

References

Baker, P. (2006). *Using Corpora in Discourse Analysis*. London: Continuum.

Baker, P. (2008). *Sexed Texts: Language, Gender and Sexuality*. Sheffield: Equinox.

Baker, P. (2010). *Sociolinguistics and Corpus Linguistics*. Edinburgh: Edinburgh University Press.

Baker, P. (2014). 'Bad wigs and screaming mimis': Using corpus-assisted techniques to carry out critical discourse analysis of the representation of trans people in the British press. In C. Hart and P. Cap, eds., *Contemporary Critical Discourse Studies*. London: Bloomsbury, pp. 211–36.

Baker, P. (2014). *Using Corpora to Analyse Gender*. London: Bloomsbury.

Baker, P. (2017). Sexuality. In E. Friginal, ed., *Studies in Corpus-Based Sociolinguistics*. London: Routledge, pp. 159–77.

Baker, P. and Brookes, G. (2021). Lovely nurses, rude receptionists, and patronising doctors: Determining the impact of gender stereotyping on patient feedback. In J. Angouri and J. Baxter, eds., *The Routledge Handbook of Language, Gender, and Sexuality*. Abingdon, UK: Routledge, pp. 559–71.

Baker, P., Brookes, G. and Evans, C. (2019). *The Language of Patient Feedback: A Corpus Linguistic Study of Online Health Communication*. London: Routledge.

Baxter, J. (2003). *Positioning Gender in Discourse: A Feminist Methodology*. Basingstoke: Palgrave Macmillan.

Benwell, B. and Stokoe, E. (2006). *Discourse and Identity*. Edinburgh: Edinburgh University Press.

Brezina, V., Love, R. and Aijmer, K. (2018). *Corpus Approaches to Contemporary British Speech: Sociolinguistic Studies of the Spoken BNC2014*. London: Routledge.

Brookes, G. and Baker, P. (2021). *Obesity in the News: Language and Representation in the Press*. Cambridge: Cambridge University Press.

Brookes, G. and Harvey, K. (2016). Examining the discourse of mental illness in a corpus of online advice-seeking messages. In L. Pickering, E. Friginal and S. Staples, eds., *Talking at Work: Corpus-Based Explorations of Workplace Discourse*. Basingstoke: Palgrave Macmillan, pp. 209–34.

Brookes, G. and McEnery, T. (2020). Corpus linguistics. In S. Adolphs and D. Knight, eds., *The Routledge Handbook of English Language and Digital Humanities*. London: Routledge, pp. 378–404.

Bucholtz, M. and Hall, K. (2005). Locating identity in language. In C. Llamas and D. Watt, eds., *Language and Identities*. Edinburgh: Edinburgh University Press, pp. 18–28.

Burr, V. (2003). *Social Constructionism*, 2nd ed. London: Routledge.

Butler, J. (1990). *Gender Trouble*. London: Routledge.

Cancer Research UK. (2021a). Bladder cancer incidence statistics. Online. www.cancerresearchuk.org/health-professional/cancer-statistics/statistics-by-cancer-type/bladder-cancer/incidence#heading-Zero

Cancer Research UK. (2021b). Bowel cancer incidence statistics. Online. www.cancerresearchuk.org/health-professional/cancer-statistics/statistics-by-cancer-type/bowel-cancer/incidence#heading-Zero

Cancer Research UK. (2021c). Cancer incidence by age. Online. www.cancerresearchuk.org/health-professional/cancer-statistics/incidence/age#heading-Zero

Cancer Research UK. (2022). Kidney cancer statistics. Online. www.cancerresearchuk.org/health-professional/cancer-statistics/statistics-by-cancer-type/kidney-cancer#heading-Zero

Couper-Kuhlen, E. (2007). Assessing and accounting. In E. Holt and R. Clift, eds., *Reporting on Talk: Reported Speech in Interaction*. Cambridge: Cambridge University Press, pp. 81–119.

Coupland, N. (2004). Age in social and sociolinguistic theory. In J. F. Nussbaum and J. Coupland, eds., *Handbook of Communication and Aging Research*, 2nd ed. London: Routledge, pp. 69–90.

Coupland, N., Coupland, J. and Giles, H. (1991). *Language, Society and the Elderly: Discourse, Identity, and Ageing*. Oxford: Blackwell.

Crenshaw, K. (1993). Mapping the margins: Intersectionality, identity politics, and violence against women of color. *Stanford Law Review*, **43**(6), 1241–99.

Dunning, T. (1993). Accurate methods for the statistics of surprise and coincidence. *Computational Linguistics*, **19**(1), 61–74.

Firth, R. J. (1957). *Papers in Linguistics 1934–1951*. Oxford: Oxford University Press.

Friginal, E. (2018). *Studies in Corpus-Based Sociolinguistics*. London: Routledge.

Fuchs, R. (2017). Do women (still) use more intensifiers than men? Recent change in the sociolinguistics of intensifiers in British English. *International Journal of Corpus Linguistics*, **22**(3), 345–74.

Gabrielatos, C. (2018). Keyness analysis: Nature, metrics and techniques. In C. Taylor and A. Marchi, eds., *Corpus Approaches to Discourse: A Critical Review*. London: Routledge, pp. 225–58.

Gleason, P. (1983). Identifying identity: A semantic history. *Journal of American History*, **69**(4), 910–31.

Habermas, J. (1979). *Moral Development and Ego Identity in Communication and the Evolution of Society*. London: Heinemann.

Hall, S. (1996). Who needs 'identity'? In S. Hall and P. du Gay, eds., *Questions of Cultural Identity*. London: Sage, pp. 1–17.

Hardie, A. (2012). CQPweb: Combining power, flexibility and usability in a corpus analysis tool. *International Journal of Corpus Linguistics*, **17**(3), 380–409.

Hardie, A. (2014). Log Ratio: An informal introduction. Online. http://cass .lancs.ac.uk/log-ratio-an-informal-introduction/

Harris, D. K. (2007). *Sociology of Aging*, 3rd ed. Maryland: Rowman & Littlefield Publishers.

Harvey, K. (2012). Disclosures of depression: Using corpus linguistics methods to interrogate young people's online health concerns. *International Journal of Corpus Linguistics*, **17**(3), 349–79.

Hunt, D. and Brookes, G. (2020). *Corpus, Discourse and Mental Health*. London: Bloomsbury.

Johnson, S. and Meinhof, U. H., eds. (1997). *Language and Masculinity*. Oxford: Blackwell.

Kendall, T. (2011). Corpora from a sociolinguistic perspective. *RBLA, Belo Horizonte*, **11**(2), 361–89.

Kimmel, M. S. (2000). *The Gendered Society*. Oxford: Oxford University Press.

Labov, W. (1966). *The Social Stratification of English in New York City*. Washington DC: Center for Applied Linguistics.

Laws, J., Ryder, C. and Jaworska, S. (2017). A diachronic corpus-based study into the effects of age and gender on the usage patterns of verb-forming suffixation in spoken British English. *International Journal of Corpus Linguistics*, **22**(3), 375–402.

McEnery, T. (2005). *Swearing in English*. London: Routledge.

McEnery, T., Baker, P. and Hardie, A. (2000). Assessing claims about language use with corpus data: Swearing and abuse. In J. M. Kirk, ed., *Corpora Galore*. Amsterdam: Rodopi, pp. 45–55.

McEnery, T. and Wilson, A. (2001). *Corpus Linguistics: An Introduction*, 2nd ed. Edinburgh: Edinburgh University Press.

Murphy, B. (2010). *Corpus and Sociolinguistics: Investigating Age and Gender in Female Talk*. Amsterdam: John Benjamins.

Myers, G. (1999). Functions of reported speech in group discussions. *Applied Linguistics*, **20**(3), 376–401.

Polanyi, L. (1979). So what's the point? *Semiotica*, **25**(3–4), 207–41.

Preece, S. (2016). Introduction: Language and identity in applied linguistics. In S. Preece, ed., *The Routledge Handbook of Language and Identity*. London: Routledge, pp. 1–16.

Rayson, P., Leech, G. and Hodges, M. (1997). Social differentiation in the use of English vocabulary: Some analyses of the conversational component of the British National Corpus. *International Journal of Corpus Linguistics*, **2**(1), 133–52.

Sacks, H. (1995). *Lectures on Conversation: Volumes 1&2*. Oxford: Blackwell.

Schegloff, E. A. (1996). Some practices for referring to persons in talk-in-interaction: a partial sketch of a systematics. In Fox, B. A. ed., *Studies in Anaphora*. Amsterdam: John Benjamins, pp. 437–85.

Sealey, A. (2009). Probabilities and surprises: A realist approach to identifying linguistic and social patterns, with reference to an oral history corpus. *Applied Linguistics*, **31**(2), 215–35.

Stubbs, M. (1996). *Texts and Corpus Analysis*. Oxford: Blackwell.

Sunderland, J. (2004). *Gendered Discourses*. Basingstoke: Palgrave Macmillan.

Swann, J. (2002). Yes, but is it gender? In L. Litosseliti and J. Sunderland, eds., *Gender Identity and Discourse Analysis*. Amsterdam: John Benjamins, pp. 43–67.

Tagliamonte, S. (2016). *Teen Talk: The Language of Adolescents*. Cambridge: Cambridge University Press.

Taylor, C. (2013). Searching for similarity using corpus-assisted discourse studies. *Corpora*, **8**(1), 81–113.

Udry, J. R. (1994). The nature of gender. *Demography*, **31**(4), 561–73.

Acknowledgements

This research was supported by ESRC Grant number LIA7835. We would like to thank Andrew Hardie for his technical assistance in preparing the corpus for analysis and Sheila Payne for her helpful insights into this project.

Cambridge Elements ⬚

Corpus Linguistics

Susan Hunston
University of Birmingham

Professor of English Language at the University of Birmingham, UK. She has been involved in Corpus Linguistics for many years and has written extensively on corpora, discourse and the lexis-grammar interface. She is probably best known as the author of *Corpora in Applied Linguistics* (2002, Cambridge University Press). Susan is currently co-editor, with Carol Chapelle, of the Cambridge Applied Linguistics series.

Advisory Board
Professor Paul Baker, *Lancaster University*
Professor Jesse Egbert, *Northern Arizona University*
Professor Gaetanelle Gilquin, *Université Catholique de Louvain*

About the Series
Corpus Linguistics has grown to become part of the mainstream of Linguistics and Applied Linguistics, as well as being used as an adjunct to other forms of discourse analysis in a variety of fields. It continues to become increasingly complex, both in terms of the methods it uses and in relation to the theoretical concepts it engages with. The Cambridge Elements in Corpus Linguistics series has been designed to meet the needs of both students and researchers who need to keep up with this changing field. The series includes introductions to the main topic areas by experts in the field as well as accounts of the latest ideas and developments by leading researchers.

Cambridge Elements ≡

Corpus Linguistics

Elements in the Series

Multimodal News Analysis across Cultures
Helen Caple, Changpeng Huan and Monika Bednarek

Doing Linguistics with a Corpus: Methodological Considerations
for the Everyday User
Jesse Egbert, Tove Larsson and Douglas Biber

Citations in Interdisciplinary Research Articles
Natalia Muguiro

Conducting Sentiment Analysis
Lei Lei and Dilin Liu

Natural Language Processing for Corpus Linguistics
Jonathan Dunn

The Impact of Everyday Language Change on the Practices of Visual Artists
Darryl Hocking

Analysing Language, Sex and Age in a Corpus of Patient Feedback:
A Comparison of Approaches
Paul Baker and Gavin Brookes

A full series listing is available at: www.cambridge.org/corpuslinguistics

Printed in the United States
by Baker & Taylor Publisher Services